Praise for

THE POWER OF giving

"One philosophy has been the cornerstone of my success in business and in life: Always be a giver—a giver of knowledge, time, wealth, and love. I am thrilled to see a book wholly dedicated to every aspect of giving.

"Azim Jamal and Harvey McKinnon do a remarkable job of addressing the all-important questions: Why give? To whom should I give? What should I give? How can I give? When should I give? With pith and wisdom they make a compelling case for the old adage that the more you give, the more you receive.

"If everyone followed the advice given in this wonderful book, our world would be a richer, more equitable, and peaceful place. I am personally touched by their deep message. I strongly believe and practice the art of giving and encourage everyone to do the same. The messages in this book resonate within me. *The Power of Giving* is a must-read. Profit from reading it. Give it to everyone you love."

—Jack Canfield, author of *The Success Principles* and cocreator of the Chicken Soup for the Soul series

"Extremely impressive . . . very inspiring."

—Dr. Wayne W. Dyer, author of *The Power of Intention*

"We've needed a book like this for a long time. Now it's your turn to help. Buy it, share it, give a copy to a friend. This book could change everything."

—Seth Godin, author of *Purple Cow: Transform Your Business by Being Remarkable*

"Our destinies will ultimately be defined by what we give, not what we get. This powerful and inspiring book will help you live a far more significant life and become more the person you were meant to be."

—Robin Sharma, author of *The Monk Who Sold His Ferrari*

"Azim Jamal and Harvey McKinnon have outlined in practical terms the many different ways in which we can give to the world around us—and to ourselves in the process. . . . Those who refresh others are themselves refreshed, and with this news we can all join a chorus and sing praises for this inspiring book!"

—Stephen Post, coauthor of *Why Good Things Happen to Good People*

"We're all going to have to reach deep to solve the common problems of our world. This wonderful book will benefit both you and your community."

—Paul Loeb, author of *Soul of a Citizen* and *The Impossible Will Take a Little While*

"*The Power of Giving* is a splendid book and an exquisite introduction to the topic of giving and generosity. Harvey McKinnon and Azim Jamal's highly readable book inspires readers to make changes that will create a win-win-win for themselves, their families, and their communities. *The Power of Giving* closes the elusive gap between personal empowerment and making our world a better place."

—Tim Draimin, founding executive director, Tides Canada

"*The Power of Giving* is an authentic, inspiring, moving, and practical book about abundance, hope, and the basic truth of philanthropy: the love of humankind. Balanced perfectly, the authors shift seamlessly from reflection based in experience and supported by research, to memorable stories that illustrate their thesis, to advice about living, loving, and giving that will inspire readers in many ways. Wise, warm, and wonderful—this book belongs in every home and office."

—Kay Sprinkel Grace, coauthor of *High Impact Philanthropy*

"Harvey and Azim elicit in their marvelous, important book *The Power of Giving* the best in human beings. Their suggestions, presented with humility and grace and courage, give each of us a renewed opportunity to think about the many, endless ways in we which we all can and must be kind, compassionate, and unstinting. In their hands, this passion to serve has become, effortlessly, a contagious art form, a 'virus' as they describe it. Please read this book and share it with everyone you know."

—Dr. Michael Tobias, ecologist, author, filmmaker

"A great guide to building a more caring world. Give a copy to everyone you love."

—Ken Burnett, author of *Relationship Fundraising*

"Everyone who reads this book will quickly be affected by what the authors call 'the giving virus'—and the world will be a much better place as a result."

—Art Hister, M.D., author of *Dr. Art Hister's Guide to Living a Long and Healthy Life*

THE POWER OF giving

Jeremy P. Tarcher/Penguin
A MEMBER OF PENGUIN GROUP (USA) INC.
New York

THE POWER OF

giving

How Giving Back Enriches Us All

AZIM JAMAL and
HARVEY McKINNON

JEREMY P. TARCHER/PENGUIN
Published by the Penguin Group
Penguin Group (USA) Inc., 375 Hudson Street, New York, New York 10014, USA •
Penguin Group (Canada), 90 Eglinton Avenue East, Suite 700, Toronto,
Ontario M4P 2Y3, Canada (a division of Pearson Canada Inc.) • Penguin Books Ltd,
80 Strand, London WC2R 0RL, England • Penguin Ireland, 25 St Stephen's Green,
Dublin 2, Ireland (a division of Penguin Books Ltd) • Penguin Group (Australia),
250 Camberwell Road, Camberwell, Victoria 3124, Australia (a division of Pearson Australia
Group Pty Ltd) • Penguin Books India Pvt Ltd, 11 Community Centre, Panchsheel Park,
New Delhi–110 017, India • Penguin Group (NZ), 67 Apollo Drive, Rosedale,
North Shore 0632, New Zealand (a division of Pearson New Zealand Ltd) • Penguin Books
(South Africa) (Pty) Ltd, 24 Sturdee Avenue, Rosebank, Johannesburg 2196, South Africa

Penguin Books Ltd, Registered Offices: 80 Strand, London WC2R 0RL, England

Most Tarcher/Penguin books are available at special quantity discounts for bulk purchase for sales
promotions, premiums, fund-raising, and educational needs. Special books or book excerpts also can
be created to fit specific needs. For details, write Penguin Group (USA) Inc. Special Markets, 375
Hudson Street, New York, NY 10014.

Library of Congress Cataloging-in-Publication Data

Jamal, Azim.
    The power of giving : how giving back enriches us all / Azim Jamal and Harvey McKinnon.
        p.   cm.
    ISBN 978-1-58542-668-3
    1. Generosity.   2. Charity.   3. Benevolence.   I. McKinnon, Harvey.   II. Title.
    BJ1533.G4J36   2008   2008018510
    177'.7—dc22

Printed in the United States of America
10 9 8 7 6 5 4 3 2 1

Book design by Jennifer Ann Daddio

We dedicate this book to all those who give—
of time, of wisdom, of wealth, and of love.

And to our families, for the joy they give us:

AZIM: farzana, sahar, tawfiq

HARVEY: marcia, james, ian

acknowledgments

To write any book involves the generosity of many people: our friends who make helpful comments, our heroes who inspire us, those who support us in many ways. Over the twenty-one months it took us to complete *The Power of Giving*, many people contributed to making this book a reality. We fear we may miss thanking someone who helped, so we first want to thank everyone who helped make *The Power of Giving* possible.

Our first-edition editor, Audrey McClellan, made the book cleaner and leaner. Thanks also to Johanna Vondeling, Sharon Boglari, Nancy Painter, Roy Bendor, Lynne Boardman, Nicky Brinkhoff, Kim Buschert, Michele Davidson, Renee Eaton,

Shannon Johnston, Allan McDonald, Tracy Vaughan, François Trahan, and Rachel Zant for their wisdom.

A prime example of "the power of giving" is the generosity of the people who helped put the first edition of the book and Web site together. Our special thanks to Merle Kamin, Melanie Bitner, Rolf Maurer, Carellin Brooks, Paul Culling, and especially Doug Forster and Radiant Communications, who made a special contribution by donating the Web site design and hosting.

We will give away a portion of our authors' profits from book sales to charities through the highly respected Tides Foundation (U.S.) and Tides Canada Foundation. So our sincere thanks to Tim Draimin and all the folks at Tides for their great work. Two other friends whose lifelong commitment to philanthropy deserves special recognition are Carol Newell and Joel Solomon. Many thanks for all that you do. You are an inspiration.

The reason you hold this edition in your hands is thanks to our agent, Donna de Guitus at the McBride Agency. She is an angel. Her support over the years has been both generous and amazing. Our editor at Penguin, Gabrielle Moss, has also been a delight to work with. Her enthusiasm for this book has been wonderful. To the other staff at Penguin who have worked on this book (and therefore are promoting "giving") we greatly appreciate the work you do.

To the generous souls who will spread the word about this book, and the ideas contained therein, thank you in advance.

To the many great nonprofit staff we have worked with over the years, thanks for the work you do, the passion you bring to your work, and the positive change you have brought to our communities.

Our deep appreciation goes to Paul Brainerd, Maria Luisa

Chea, Carlie, Lynette and Russ Lewis, Mr. and Mrs. Raj Naidu, Craig O'Brien, Jenny Oad, Salim Premji, Eleanor Ryrie, Severn Suzuki, Peggy Taylor, Hussain Tejany, Joy Trek, Caroline Van Nostrand, David Van Seters, and Michael Nicoll Yahgulanaas for your inspiring stories.

To our wonderful families, who have helped teach us that when you give from the heart it all comes back with interest. From Harvey, thanks to Marcia, James, Ian, Carole, Jan, Greg, Brenda, Claire, Brian, Moira, Yuichi, Cindy, Bob, Kristen, Hussain, Todd, and to his parents, James and Evelyn. And from Azim, thanks to Farzana, Sahar, Tawfiq, Mehboob, Shaffin, and to his parents, Abdul and Shirin.

contents

preface 1

introduction 7

The Power of Giving 10

Why We Wrote This Book 11

Who Should Read This Book? 13

How This Book Is Organized 14

How You Can Use This Book 14

Our Gift to You 15

CHAPTER 1

why give?   17

Gifts Were Given to You   18

The Benefits of Giving   19

   New Relationships   20

   Reduction of Fears   21

   Good Health   22

   Living to Your Potential   23

   Maslow's Hierarchy of Needs   25

   Finding Meaning, Fulfillment, and Happiness   28

   The More You Give of Yourself, the More You Find of Yourself   30

Giving Is a Beautiful Experience   32

Key Points   34

CHAPTER 2

what can you give?   35

Love   37

   Love Isn't Always Easy   38

   What Love Is Not   40

   Making Time for Love   41

   Expressing Love   42

Laughter   44

   Tragically Funny?   45

Knowledge   48

   Take Away the TV   51

Education and Lifelong Learning 52

Intelligence and Wisdom 53

Leadership 54

Corporate Leadership 57

Hope 59

Life 60

Time 62

How Are You Spending Your Time? 64

Money 64

How Are Your Attitudes to Money? 65

How Do You Feel About Money? 66

Do You Know the Difference Between "Want" and "Need"? 67

Managing Money 69

Skills 70

Sharing Skills 71

Building Skills to Give 72

What New Skills Do You Want to Develop? 73

Health 75

Touch 75

Attention 77

Advice 78

Giving What You Need Most 81

Balance 82

Key Points 84

CHAPTER 3

to whom should you give?

85

Start with Yourself   86

    Listening to Your Inner Voice   87

    Give Yourself a Break   88

    Learning the Hard Way   90

    The First Step to Helping Yourself   91

Giving to Your Family   92

    Giving to Your Spouse   93

    Healing Relationships   96

    How Healthy Are Your Relationships?   99

    Giving to Your Children   99

    Teaching Giving to Your Children   101

    Giving Your Children Heart Fiber   104

Community   105

    Giving to Elders   109

    The Broader Community   110

    Giving Globally   112

    Giving to Nonprofit Social Organizations   114

    Types of Nonprofit Groups   116

    Small Organizations Can Have a Big Impact   117

Giving to Our Planet   119

Key Points   123

CHAPTER 4

how, when, where, and how much to give

125

How to Give   126

    Give with Respect   127

    Give with Humility   128

    Give Unconditionally   129

When to Give   130

    Giving in Hardship   131

Where to Give   133

    Emotions, Values, and Motivations   133

    Why Do I Want to Give?   134

    Skills   135

    What Nonprofits Need Most   136

    What Other Resources Can You Offer?   138

    Putting It All Together   138

    Evaluating Nonprofits   140

How Much to Give   142

    Living a Simpler Life   143

    Tithing   145

       Money Tithing   145

       Time Tithing   146

       Idea Tithing   147

       Intrapersonal Tithing   148

    Escalator Giving   151

Planned Giving 153

Giving for the Big Picture 153

Key Points 156

CHAPTER 5

corporate giving 157

Giving to Customers 158

Giving to Employees 161

Giving to the Community 163

Giving to the Environment 164

Giving from the Bottom Up 167

Key Points 168

CHAPTER 6

giving up 169

A Final Word 172

Will You Help? 173

Key Points 174

resource list 175

index 181

preface

In late December 2004 a natural disaster precipitated the largest humanitarian aid operation in history.

The South Asian tsunami killed hundreds of thousands of people and left more than a million others homeless. The disaster ripped families apart. Children lost their parents; parents lost their children. In some families, only one person survived.

The shocking power of nature and the devastation of the tsunami caused another incredible reaction: a worldwide desire to help the survivors. Hundreds of thousands of people living in the affected countries fed their neighbors, gave them shelter, and comforted them in their grief. Foreign visitors ended their beach holidays as volunteers, picking up corpses and trying to help identify the dead. Across the world, tens of millions of individuals responded to the tragedy by sending immediate donations to aid agencies. Governments responded to their citizens and contributed massive aid for reconstruction. The world pledged $8.5 billion. You may have made a donation yourself. More than half the citizens of many countries sent a gift.

This generous global response made a positive, life-changing difference for many people. The generosity in response to the tsunami shows how easy it is to give from the heart.

In the world today there are many "disasters" that will kill many more people than the tsunami—they just aren't as graphic, immediate, or as easy to present on TV. Often, there isn't the local angle to drive media coverage, and the locations are more remote and often dangerous for foreign media. Ethnic cleansing in Darfur, Sudan; the HIV/AIDS crisis; and preventable infant mortality are all disasters in which countless people will die. And yet each of these tragedies has inspired dedicated, courageous people to try to save lives. Like those in the tsunami-affected areas, the unknown victims of war and disease need and deserve our compassion. And we urge you to continue to expand your generosity to include them if at all possible.

You'll see in this book that we focus on a person's individual motivations and actions. So, in effect, this book was actually written for you.

We hope it reads a bit like a conversation. That it feels like we were in a room with you, perhaps drinking tea (strong coffee for Harvey), having a chat about life, about your contribution, and your future. Together we will have some laughs, share ideas, feel inspired by each other, each of us learning something from one another, as good friends do. And all three of us will come out of the conversation feeling better about ourselves and our world. Inspired to give more. Each of us can change and improve our own life. When we do so, it is certain that we will improve other lives as well.

There's one chapter in our book that you may feel has a slightly different focus than the others. It's chapter five, and it's about your workplace. At the last minute, we decided to add this chapter on corporate giving. Why? Well, most of us spend a significant portion of our lives working, perhaps one-third of our waking hours. The majority of people work at corporations. And we believe people can have an enormous impact in their workplace when they apply the ideas and principles outlined in this book. In effect, when you bring these principles to work, you will promote a healthier culture, balance, and make a greater contribution to your community.

An article, "Doing good deeds can improve health, make you happier, scientists suggest" by Erin Anderssen in the *Globe and Mail* describes a series of studies supporting our belief that giving also benefits the giver:

- One study revealed that people who exhibit higher levels of altruism get a "helper's high," a release of endorphins. This high can "give the immune system a boost, speed recovery from surgery and cut down on those restless nights."

- Thanks to new brain-scan technology, scientists have also discovered evidence that humans are "hard wired" to take care of and help each other.
- A Florida study of people with AIDS showed that those who volunteered to help others were likely to live longer than those who did not.
- A British poll of volunteers found that half of those surveyed claimed that their health had improved while they were volunteering. Twenty percent of them claimed they lost weight, too, which is a higher success rate than any diet we know. Maybe our next book will be a diet book—although maybe this book is actually a diet book and we don't know it. Let us know if you lose weight after volunteering.

We have said for a long time that over the years more research will be conducted on volunteerism, altruism, and giving. We are confident that the research will overwhelmingly confirm that giving works both ways: that the recipients benefit, as do the donors. And that is good news for all of us.

Being generous in spirit and deed is a great comfort to the soul.

Whatever we may "lose" in the moment of giving, whether it be time, money, or opportunities, will be more than matched by all we gain. We believe the gains are immense and longer lasting. They include deeper friendships, teaching others generosity, greater personal integrity, a sense of freedom, joy, and even love. As Piero Ferrucci says so eloquently, "Being kind is the simplest way to become who we really are."

When you work on developing your giving skills, it will benefit your family, your community, and yourself. We urge you to share the ideas and stories in this book (including copies of the book) as well as your own experiences in giving. Together, we believe we can build a more caring world. Thank you.

Harvey and Azim

introduction

We live in a world of violence, human suffering, and environ-mental destruction. What can we, as caring beings, do to help heal the wounds of others and reduce their pain? What can we do to heal our personal wounds and diminish our own suffering?

We can give. Everyone has something to give, be it time, money, wisdom, love, or a variety of other things.

We can accomplish miracles through our giving. Giving ideas, skills, and resources can dramatically improve the world we live in. Whatever our circumstances, we can have a positive influence on other lives. Have you ever heard the saying, "We may only be one person in the world. But we may be the world to one person"? Each of us, if we choose, can give hope, love, and healing. And the first person you need to give to might even be yourself.

We believe that giving is a fundamental human need—one that benefits both the recipients of the gift and the giver. While we are alive, giving fulfills us and taps into our innate gifts. The positive impact of giving remains long after we die, as we live on in the memories and good feelings of our friends, family, and community. All else is forgotten.

If you ever think your giving won't make a difference, please remember Carlie.

When she was three, Carlie was a perfectly healthy child. Then one day she came down with a bad fever. Her parents, Russ and Lynette, took her to the hospital only to discover every parent's nightmare: Carlie had cancer.

As the cancer treatment started, all her parents could do was pray. Then, near the end of her ten months of chemotherapy, Carlie's grandmother gave her a surprise. She asked the Make-A-Wish Foundation to grant Carlie's dream wish. The largest wish-granting organization in the world, with affiliates in twenty-two countries, the Make-A-Wish Foundation exists for one purpose: to fulfill the special wishes of children who have been diagnosed with life-threatening illnesses.

Three weeks before Carlie received her dream wish, which was to go to Sea World, she came down with pneumonia and influenza. Six days later, Carlie was in a coma. The doctors told Russ and Lynette that she had a 20 percent chance of surviving. Carlie grew worse. After seventeen days in a coma, she had lost 98 percent of her lung capacity. She was paralyzed and had thirteen tubes in her tiny body. The doctors told her parents she would not live through the weekend. Russ later recalled, "I don't know if you can imagine how horrible it was to hear this news. Our baby was dying."

The nurses, who had been told to say good-bye to Carlie on Friday at the end of their shift, were shocked to see Russ still there on Monday morning. But a miracle had happened. Carlie had regained consciousness. She had lost half her body weight—but she was alive. Just twelve days later, Carlie was carried onto a plane to fly to Sea World. She was going to get her wish to swim with dolphins. When Carlie returned after two weeks, she had the strength to run into her grandmother's arms. Carlie's recovery was amazing.

Today, five years later, Carlie is a healthy and energetic child. Russ understandably believes he is one of the luckiest people on earth. He feels that his dying child was given life, and he says, "I believe it's because she wanted her wish so badly that she came back from heaven to get it. When you're as sick as Carlie was, the only thing that could get you out of bed is a dream—something you desperately wish for.

"I know we were lucky. I know that many kids won't get a chance to live long lives. But they can have their most cherished wish fulfilled. And as a parent who almost lost a child, I can tell you that you will be giving a wonderful—and very important—gift."

Carlie's wish was granted because approximately one hundred seventy generous donors sent money to the Make-A-Wish Foundation. They had never met Carlie. They gave without knowing her story, hoping only to help a sick child, and they gave a gift of life. Now Russ and his wife are giving back by volunteering for Make-A-Wish. They also regularly share *their* story of the power of giving—to help raise more money for more children.

Carlie's story shows that you have the power to give happiness and perhaps even life to children in your own community or thousands of miles away. It only takes the power of your will and your heart.

There are many more—millions more—stories of life-changing gifts that people have generously given to others. Some involve money, others time; all involve compassion and love.

In this book, we hope to inspire you to start giving or to increase what you already give, for we truly believe that you, as well as others, will benefit greatly.

the power of giving

Giving creates a symbiotic relationship; it benefits both parties. The recipients benefit from your gift. And you benefit personally by virtue of having been a giver. Sometimes it is easy to see the immediate benefits to those you help. Other times, the ultimate benefits of your action may occur many years in the future. It could be that your gift helps the sick, funds a project for your favorite charity, or helps a child learn something valuable. Whatever your gift, your time, money, or effort will have a positive impact.

The other side of the equation is the benefits to you. They may be visible and immediate, or they may be intangible and delayed. You may not even recognize them as benefits. You may gain a tax deduction. You may feel great about your ability to help. You may receive heartfelt thanks. You may see the preservation of something you believe in or change in an area where you have been seeking it.

Whatever form the benefits take, giving brings meaning to

your life. When you give, you have a chance to make an incredible impact during and often beyond your life. And when you give without expecting a return, you reap even more benefits.

Our personal experience has been that the more we give, the more excitement, energy, and pleasure we derive from our lives. When individuals give, they take important steps on the road to achieving their personal potential—all the while improving the world through their actions.

why we wrote this book

Both of us have been lucky to receive many opportunities to give, which we consider a blessing. In our many years of service we have experienced growth, joy, abundance, and the power of giving.

For the past twenty-five years, Azim has spent an average of twenty hours a week in voluntary work. He has been the chair of many volunteer organizations, ranging from social welfare boards to youth organizations. He has traveled extensively to Africa, Europe, Australia, New Zealand, the United States, and Asia on assignments for these organizations. He has had many opportunities to serve in war-torn and disaster-stricken places, including helping Afghan refugees in Pakistan. Before Azim became a professional speaker, he gave several hundred inspirational talks around the world in a voluntary capacity, talking about "life balance," which included the power of giving.

Azim learned to serve from his parents and grandparents. As far back as he can remember, he saw them give tirelessly of their time, money, and wisdom to one and all. They did it with a great sense of humility and gratitude that came naturally to them. This left an indelible impression on Azim.

Harvey has worked on "giving issues" for more than thirty years and has been a volunteer with dozens of nonprofits during that time. He's done everything from stuffing envelopes and washing dishes to sitting on national boards of some of the largest global nonprofits. He decided decades ago to dedicate his skills to nonprofits that work on social justice issues, environmental protection, and helping people live better lives. He also donates to many causes and shares his ideas and his time with people working to build better and more caring communities. He has studied giving and has trained thousands of staff people and volunteers from nonprofits active in more than fifty countries.

One of the reasons we became authors and trainers is that we both love learning, acquiring knowledge, and passing it on to others when we think it will help them. We are what Malcolm Gladwell describes in his book *The Tipping Point* as "mavens," people who absorb information and feel compelled to share it with others. This can have an obnoxious side. Looking back, we both see times in our youth when we were certain that our analysis and experiences were the only way, and of course we shared our views with everyone we met. The arrogance of youth became somewhat tempered as we hit the fifty-year mark. Today we are both wiser and more willing to admit that we make mistakes and that we still have lots to learn. However, we retain the energy and enthusiasm for passing on to others the knowledge that we hope will be helpful.

We both have received fantastic benefits from the power of giving, so we wanted to share our experience with others. We felt that by our working together, the resulting synergy would produce a book that would make a difference in the world. We want to

- share with you the importance and the power of giving;
- highlight that even a small amount of regular giving can significantly improve your relationships, productivity, and happiness;
- show you how to have a greater impact with your giving;
- show that most people can give a little more and that there are enormous benefits when they do so; and
- emphasize that if everyone gave a little more, our world would be a more peaceful, healthier, and happier place.

who should read this book?

At the risk of sounding overambitious, we believe that everyone should read this book. Even if you aren't wealthy, you surely have time, skills, knowledge, or assets that you can give to others. We hope *The Power of Giving* will inspire all readers, from the person who currently gives a lot to the person who gives nothing.

We want to reassure people who already give a lot that even though at times they may feel frustrated, their giving is still noticed and rewarded. We encourage these people to balance their lives, to learn to receive as well as to give, and to give to their families, the less privileged, and of course themselves.

We hope to inspire those people who currently give nothing to begin the journey of giving by showing them how this process creates a ripple effect that will return many benefits to them—benefits ranging from inner happiness to the chance to achieve their true potential.

how this book is organized

As we worked on this book, it seemed to flow naturally from the sometimes abstract benefits of giving to the nitty-gritty detail of deciding how much to give and whom to give it to.

In chapter one we explain why you should give, showing the benefits you and others receive from it.

Our second chapter focuses on what you can give, whether it be tangible items like time and money, or less concrete gifts like love, hope, or leadership.

In the third chapter we discuss whom you can give to—yourself, your family, and your community, or a broader target such as refugees on another continent or the entire planet.

Our fourth chapter focuses on how, when, where, and how much you can give. This chapter includes discussions on giving in hardship, tithing, and how to plan your giving.

Finally, we end the book with a chapter on "giving up" and a request that you personally promote giving among your friends and community.

how you can use this book

We encourage you to read the book cover to cover, highlighting areas that you want to spend more time on.

Also, we suggest you read a page or two at random every night before you go to sleep and first thing in the morning (a few minutes per day). This random reading starts your day with uplifting thoughts that linger in your subconscious mind as you go about your day.

our gift to you

We hope that this book will help you become a better giver—more generous, more strategic—and that you in turn will help others to become better givers too. We believe that if we can encourage and motivate more people to give others their time, knowledge, resources, and kindness, our world will be a more peaceful and happier place.

We hope we can inspire you to become more involved in your community and to be more generous with your time and money. We hope you'll be one of those special people who make a major difference, whether to one life or to many. This book is our gift to you and to all those who read it.

why give?

There's no denying that life in the twenty-first century is demanding. There never seems to be enough time to do all the things that need to be done: keep up with work or studies, spend time with family, earn enough money to pay the rent and buy necessities. With so many challenges to cope with, you may ask yourself, "Why should I expend any effort in giving?" or "I'm already scrambling to deal with all the demands and pressures on me. How will I find time and resources to give more?" or "No one gives to me, so why should I give to others?"

In this chapter we hope to show you that no matter what your circumstances in life, you have the ability to give. As well, giving is good for you. It provides the following benefits:

- It can make a positive difference to others.
- There are emotional, physical, and even financial benefits to you.
- It can help you achieve your full potential.
- It can bring you more meaning, fulfillment, and happiness.

gifts were given to you

Probably the biggest gift you will ever receive is the huge investment your parents made in you. But they are not the only ones who have given to you. During the course of your life you have received many things from other people—teachers, relatives, strangers. Schools and hospitals were built with the hard work and tax dollars of those who preceded you. In fact, almost everything you use in your life has been made by someone else. The peace that you enjoy has been delivered by the sacrifice of others. When you think about it, you know countless people who have made a difference in your life—some negative, some positive. Why not make a decision to have a positive impact on the lives of others, even if they are strangers?

Consider the following statistics:

- One out of every four people in the world is starving.
- As many as 1.5 billion people in the world do not have enough clean water.
- At least 20 million people are suffering the horror of war, imprisonment, and torture.

- Every few seconds a child dies from a preventable disease.
- One-seventh of the world's population is illiterate.
- In the United States, the world's richest country, 3 million people are homeless each year.

There are also great needs within your own community. In the face of such need and desperation, you have two choices: you can decide to help others and change lives, or you can decide to do nothing and lose the benefits of giving. But remember, when people come together to tackle a difficult situation, they receive far more than they can ever imagine.

the benefits of giving

What are those benefits of giving? Here are some of the things you can gain by making giving a greater part of your life:

- new relationships
- a feeling of security
- jobs
- good health
- a sense of empowerment, pride, and accomplishment
- happiness
- peace and love

The paradox is that when you give expecting a reward, you won't receive one. When you give with joy, selflessness, and love, you benefit greatly. The attitude you bring to your giving will reflect the benefits you gain. Parents share their shelter, food, and love with their children simply because they love them and not because they seek their love. Ultimately, the rewards are tremendous. Yet if you give money, time, or anything else with an expectation of a return on your investment, you defeat the purpose of giving. This can be a negative lesson: you gave and you didn't feel any better. This lack of "emotional reward" can lead to not wanting to give. Then you lose, as do those you could be helping.

NEW RELATIONSHIPS

Psychologists who study babies know that they (like all human beings) crave interaction with other humans. In fact, babies who are not nurtured by their parents or other caregivers wither emotionally from lack of bonding. Many of them never recover.

We believe that this is also true of adults. If adults lack stimulating interaction with others, their souls shrink. Really, it's only through connecting with other human beings that you learn about the world, about yourself, and even about your destiny. After all, other people are a mirror in which you can see yourself. This interconnection enables you to reach your full potential and to strengthen your soul.

The Trappist monk Thomas Merton once wrote: "Souls are like athletes who need opponents worthy of them if they are to be tried and extended and pushed to the full use of their powers." That's an insightful analogy, for just as your muscles weaken without physical exercise, so does your soul weaken without its special kinds of exercise. A great exercise for your soul is the practice of giving. As with physical exercise, the more you do it, the easier it is, and the stronger you will become.

REDUCTION OF FEARS

Giving can also reduce your fears. That's because giving promotes social connections, which provide you with greater security.

Do you live in fear of economic disaster? Do you worry about caring for your parents or putting your children through college? Do you worry about losing your good health? Do you fear that crime, war, or terrorist attacks will disrupt the economy and your security? These are legitimate concerns that many people share. We live in difficult and uncertain times, but are these fears real?

Research shows that people who watch a lot of news on television overestimate the threats to their well-being. Why? Because television focuses on news that makes the world seem like a more dangerous place than it actually is. Afraid of the world that is portrayed on TV, people "cocoon," staying in their homes with close family, and do not build bonds with their neighbors. Thus, they become more vulnerable.

The best way to confront your fears is to begin the process of making a difference. The root causes of "dangers" are often the result of social problems that have been ignored. But you can make a commitment to do what you can to eliminate the conditions that cause the potential crises. By facing your fears and working to change their root causes, you overcome them.

Giving is a key part of this process because giving reduces self-centeredness. It can make you feel more connected to others, and this connection will reduce fear and isolation. Author Robert Putnam's massive research project, which culminated in the book *Bowling Alone*, clearly demonstrates the benefits to staying connected with others—for security, health, happiness, and even income.

Have you ever heard of a job opportunity through a personal connection? Have you ever had neighbors help you out during a difficult situation? Has a friend ever cared for your child when you were exhausted?

These are just a few of the benefits that occur when you are connected with other people. The list is endless.

GOOD HEALTH

Academic research demonstrates that giving to others benefits people physically and emotionally. An article in the May 1988 issue of *American Health* magazine described a study in Michigan that showed that regular volunteer work increases life expectancy. The study found that men who did no volunteer work were two and a half times more likely to die during the study than men who volunteered at least once a week. The article described other benefits that the researchers measured.

Giving, in the form of volunteer work:

- enhances your immune system,
- lowers cholesterol levels,
- strengthens your heart,
- decreases the incidence of chest pains, and
- generally reduces stress.

The world can be a different and better place if, while you are here, you give of yourself. This concept became clear to Azim one day when he was watching television at an airport terminal while waiting for a flight. A priest was sharing a story about newborn twins, one of whom was ill. The twins were in separate incubators, as per hospital rules. A nurse on the floor repeatedly suggested that the twins be kept together in one incubator. The doctors finally agreed to try this. When the twins were brought into contact with each other, the healthy twin immediately put his arms around his sick brother. This instinctive exchange gradually helped the sick twin to recover and regain his health. The babies' family and the doctors witnessed the intangible force of love and the incredible power of giving.

LIVING TO YOUR POTENTIAL

Rumi, a thirteenth-century Persian mystic, told of a man who walked past a beggar and asked, "Why, God, do you not do something for these people?" God replied, "I did do something. I made you."

When Rumi wrote these words, he was addressing our ability to choose what we do, our ability to reach our potential.

Most people use only a tiny portion of their potential, and many never find their true gift or calling in life. They never find a worthwhile cause to support, a cause that really means something to them and makes a difference in their lives.

But when you give to others or give of yourself to meaningful causes, things change. You expect more of yourself. You discover new feelings of self-worth. Indeed, you begin to tap into your true gifts and talents. And when you do that, you can achieve your full potential as you help yourself and others.

Until 1997 Azim was a professional accountant. In 1993 he also became head of his community's social welfare board, where he volunteered twenty to twenty-five hours a week. This work led to an invitation to develop a budget for Focus, a humanitarian agency. He accepted the invitation and went to spend several weeks with Afghan refugees in Pakistan.

While in Pakistan, Azim saw many things that shook his soul. One instance, in particular, was his visit to an Afghan refugee camp, where he heard stories about how the refugees lived through war after war. Fleeing from Afghanistan with only the clothes they wore, a few of them had even seen their fathers being killed in front of their eyes. Some worked fourteen hours a day, making only a dollar a day. Azim met Afghan children who were the same age as his own children. It made him think, "What if my children were in this predicament?" He had heard the statement that we are all interconnected, but for the first time he actually felt what this statement meant. As he was riding back to his hotel in a cab, he sobbed like a baby.

That night he could not sleep. He tossed and turned, asking himself how he could really help these people. Finally, he realized that he would not be able to make a big impact as a professional accountant because he was not passionate about accounting. In this night of grief and pain, he made a decision to pursue his gift of inspirational speaking and writing. That day in the Afghan refugee camp was a life-altering experience for Azim.

As Mahatma Gandhi said, "To find yourself, lose yourself in the service of others." Azim believes that by losing himself in his voluntary work during that trip, he found himself and got closer to achieving his full potential.

maslow's hierarchy of needs

Some people claim they can't give because they haven't yet achieved a certain level of self-actualization. They may be basing their claim on Abraham Maslow's famous hierarchy of needs. Maslow was a psychologist who studied human motivation, leading him to create a pyramid showing what people need to be fulfilled.

The base of Maslow's pyramid starts with our core physiological needs: air, water, food, shelter, warmth, sleep, sex, and so on. The second level comprises our security needs: protection from the elements, social order, law, and so on. The third level includes our social needs: love, family, relationships, work group, and so on. The fourth level consists of our ego needs: achievement, reputation, responsibility, independence, prestige, status, and so on.

Maslow originally placed self-actualization needs at the top of his five-stage model. These needs were satisfied through personal growth, self-fulfillment, and the resolution of personal potential. Later models placed self-actualization as a seventh stage (above two new levels: cognitive needs—knowledge, meaning, and self-awareness—and aesthetic needs—beauty, balance, and form). Others have added an eighth and final level: our spiritual needs, achieved through transcendence and helping others to achieve self-actualization.

Maslow believed that needs must be satisfied in the order

(continued)

of the levels he described. He felt that only after a level had been reached could an individual begin to work on meeting the next level of needs.

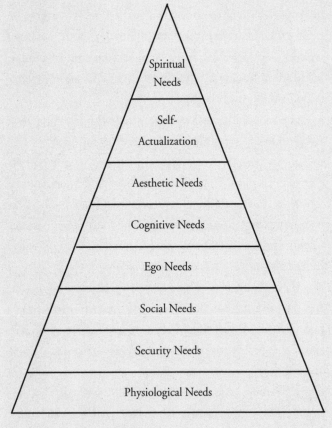

MASLOW'S HIERARCHY OF NEEDS

While we believe Maslow's hierarchy of needs is funda- mentally sound, we've seen enough positive signs to know that people can aspire to, and meet, some needs above a level they have not fully achieved. For example, it may be that a person struggling at level three (social needs) may discover that through knowledge (level five), he or she can satisfy some of his level three and four social and ego needs.

We also believe that every human being deserves the opportunity to reach self-actualization and to realize his or her potential. Your giving will help you and many other people come closer to their potential.

And, finally, we believe that self-actualization will not happen unless most, if not all, of the lower levels are achieved. Therefore, to reduce violence, promote equality, and increase people's fulfillment, we believe we should help people to meet their basic physiological and safety needs. With millions of people in the Western world lacking the means to satisfy their basic needs, and more than a billion worldwide living in similar conditions, there is a lot of work to do. As you may know, there is adequate food, water, and resources to support and shelter every human in the world. But the way they are distributed is obviously unequal. When you help others to meet their needs, you increase the likelihood of meeting your own needs.

When you strive to develop Maslow's self-actualization characteristics (see diagram), you will bring much joy into your life. These characteristics will confer on you more wisdom, stronger relationships, greater compassion, and internal peace. If you achieve self-actualization, you will be able

(continued)

to see situations with more objectivity and clarity. You will see problems as challenges and as growth opportunities. You will not rely on culture and the environment to form your opinions. You will be able to protect your inner values. You will believe in justice. You will be able to embrace and enjoy all races, cultures, faiths, and differences. You will be accepting, understanding, and compassionate. You will be able to laugh at yourself and the human condition. You will seek experiences that are deep, meaningful, and lasting.

We believe that as you become a more generous and thoughtful giver, you will also develop some or all of these gifts.

FINDING MEANING, FULFILLMENT, AND HAPPINESS

All people want to achieve meaning, fulfillment, and happiness. However, thousands of years of human history confirm that these things come not from being self-centered but rather from making a difference and giving happiness to others. Mother Teresa is a famous example. She found fulfillment when she helped change the expression on dying people's faces from distress and fear to calmness and serenity. By giving herself to others, she made their undeniable pain a little easier to bear.

The Sufi Nasruddin (a Sufi is a Muslim spiritualist and wise person) tells the story of a person who is drowning. People shouted at the man, "Give us your hand so we can save you!" But the man was hesitant. Finally, someone said to the man, "Take my hand," and the man took it. This man was more familiar with taking than giving. He almost died as a result.

If you find yourself feeling unhappy, try making someone else happy and see what happens. If you are feeling empty and unfulfilled, try doing some meaningful and worthwhile work and see how you feel.

The catch is that you must do this work with passion and enthusiasm. If you are not passionate, it is hard to produce good work. You are less likely to feel fulfilled and happy or to believe your work is meaningful. In the end, you will lose energy for the work, leaving you with poor results.

There is a story of an elderly carpenter who was ready to retire. The carpenter told his employer of his plans to leave the house-building business and live a more leisurely life with his wife, enjoying his extended family. The employer was sorry to see his employee go and asked if he would build just one more house as a personal favor to him. The carpenter reluctantly agreed. He did sloppy work and he used inferior materials. It was an unfortunate way to end a dedicated career.

When the carpenter finished his work, the employer came to inspect the house. Then he handed the front-door key to the carpenter. "This is your house," he said. "It is my retirement gift to you." The carpenter was shocked. If he had only known he was building his own house, he would have done it all so differently.

So it is with all people. Every person builds his or her own house, his or her own life, a step at a time, often half-heartedly. Then with a shock they realize they have to live in the house they have built. If they could do it over, they'd do it differently. But they cannot go back.

You are the carpenter; your life is your building project. When you treat others in the way you wish to be treated, you are building with love and care. Always do your best because the choices you make today build your future.

THE MORE YOU GIVE OF YOURSELF, THE MORE YOU FIND OF YOURSELF

"A rich life," writes philosopher and theologian Cornel West, "consists fundamentally of serving others, trying to leave the world a little better than you found it." Every one of us can have a rich life if we choose.

If you are wealthy but unable to share your wealth or give of your possessions and knowledge, you are not really rich. Conversely, if you are not wealthy but give of your self, your time, and your knowledge, you are indeed quite rich—and you will receive far more than you can ever imagine.

Mahatma Gandhi once said, "There is always enough for the needy but never enough for the greedy." Have you ever noticed how the needy frequently find a way to be grateful for the very little they have, whereas the greedy never seem to have enough?

If you are worth billions of dollars and have no people or causes to give your money to, what do you do with your money? How many houses can you live in? How many cars can you drive? How many meals can you eat? And even if you indulge in all of these things to excess, what do you do with the rest of your money?

There is a story of a wealthy businessman who never gave anything to anyone. A tenacious fund-raiser approached the man to ask for a gift to a charitable cause, but the man refused to contribute. After much persuasion, the fund-raiser eventually asked the wealthy man to pick up some good dirt from his garden and hand it to him as his gift. Wanting to get rid of the fund-raiser and knowing the dirt was free, the man picked it up and gave it to the fund-raiser, who then left. A few days later, the wealthy man, who was now curious, asked the fund-raiser why he had asked for the dirt. The fund-raiser explained, "I wanted you to taste the beauty of giving, even though it is only dirt you were giving. Once you taste the beauty of giving something small, you will eventually give something big."

Of course, it would have helped if the miserly man from our story understood that the more you give, the more you receive. This may sound like a paradox—but it's true. The more you give of yourself, the more you find of yourself. When you make a positive difference in the lives of others, you make a positive difference in your own life. Giving is a "win-win" proposition.

Author Earl Nightingale tells a story of a man who went to his empty fireplace and said, "Give me heat and I'll give you the wood." But giving does not work that way. In fact, giving functions under the universal law of cause and effect. You need to work for the wood before you get the heat. In other words, our rewards will always match and follow our service or, in the words of the Bible, You will always reap what you sow.

"When all is said and done," says author Og Mandino, "success without happiness is the worst kind of failure."

How can you find that happiness? It all comes back to giving. If you want to have happiness, you need to give happiness. If you want wealth, you need to give wealth. If you want love, you need to give love. For it is only in giving that you receive. Giving enriches your life with meaning, fulfillment, and happiness. It allows you to unleash your potential and create breakthroughs. In fact, it is a privilege to give. So give of your time, your knowledge, your wisdom, your wealth, and your love—and experience the power and beauty of giving.

giving is a beautiful experience

We want to end this chapter with two stories about the beauty of giving.

A kindly stranger had a profound effect on Azim's cousin Salim when he was in the hospital a few years ago. Salim was both sick and depressed when one day a woman he didn't know visited him. She noticed that the flowers in his room were unkempt and asked Salim, "Do you mind if I fix the flowers for you?" He said, "Of course not." She came back with the flowers, beautifully rearranged. Then she made him a cup of tea. Her actions touched his heart, and Salim started to come out of his doldrums. The two of them became friends.

Not long after, the woman's husband died, and Salim was able to comfort her. Their friendship has been a pillar of support for each of them, but it was only after she gave freely that Salim was moved to give back freely to her too.

The second story also takes place in a hospital. Each holiday season you can see thousands and thousands of paper doves hanging suspended in the atrium of Toronto's Princess Margaret Hospital, one of the world's leading cancer research centers. It's a magical sight. The dove is a symbol of hope. Each dove honors a person lost to cancer or living with cancer, or a special person who helped someone with his or her battle against cancer.

Caroline van Nostrand, who works for the Princess Margaret Hospital Foundation, organizes the Dove fund-raising campaign. Two years ago, during the Dove dedication ceremony, a man named David approached Caroline as she was standing in the atrium. David told her that he had dedicated a dove in memory of his wife, Nancy, who died of cancer. He told Caroline he was touched by the holiday season campaign, and he asked her if he could have his dove returned to him—to remember the event and the spirit of his contribution. Her eyes filled with tears when David told her about his wife. But she also felt it would be impossible to find Nancy's dove amid the thousands of others in the atrium. She told David she would try but warned him that he would likely have to wait until all the doves were taken down.

About fifteen minutes later, David approached Caroline again and told her that since Nancy had died, he had felt her presence in his daily life. He told Caroline that he still talked to her and sought her counsel from time to time. On this particular afternoon, he stood in the middle of the atrium and asked silently, "Nancy, where's our dove?" To Caroline's amazement, less than thirty seconds later—and from among more than forty-five hundred doves—he found Nancy's. David said that his wife had led him right to it.

Caroline says, "It's stories like this that make my work here so rewarding. Stories like these that make our doves so important for people living with cancer."

At the core of all giving is compassion and love—and it grows when you become a better giver.

Ask yourself: When I give, how do I feel? Do I feel energized, happy, and fulfilled? Or do I feel deprived, shortchanged, and less well off? What are my past experiences with giving? Were they happy or sad? What has been my best experience of giving? What has been my worst experience of giving?

Your responses to the questions above will give you some clarity about how you feel about giving. We hope that by reading this chapter you'll be encouraged to continue to give irrespective of your past experiences.

key points

There is much sadness in the world, but there are also unlimited ways to make a positive difference.

You can gain tremendous benefits from giving. Among these benefits are new friends, a feeling of security, better health, happiness, and a sense of pride. You are at your best when you make a difference and contribute.

Passion for a worthwhile cause helps you tap into your creativity.

You need only so much as an individual to be happy. Therefore, to live to your potential and create abundance, you need to do something larger than yourself—thus the need to give.

You are a conduit—the more you allow giving to flow through you, the more abundance flows back into your life. The more you give, the more you receive.

Giving is a beautiful experience.

what can you give?

You may have much to give, or you may have only a little to give. The key to the power of giving is giving to your potential. The first step toward reaching your potential is determining what you have that could be of value to others. You may have more than you think.

First, you should assess what your skills, abilities, and resources are. They could include time, money, or the ability to organize a fund-raising event, or they could be more intangible, like love, wisdom, and attention. It may be that random acts of kindness are all that you can give at this point in your life. Offering neighbors vegetables from your garden is a great gift, as is calling a distant relative just to say hello, or learning juggling so you can entertain kids. Giving doesn't have to cost a lot in time or money.

Keep in mind that your actions have implications, usually positive, beyond your original gift. The recipient of your extra carrots may think, "I can share my surplus with others too," just as the distant relative may be inspired by your thoughtful gesture to connect with others. Kindness is a wonderful form of giving.

This ability to stimulate others to give was dramatized in the movie *Pay It Forward* (adapted from Catherine Ryan Hyde's novel). This movie is about a seventh-grade student who, while completing a school assignment, comes up with a concept that could actually change the world. The concept: one person will perform three acts of kindness. Rather than expecting the three people given assistance to pay him or her back for the kindness, the person will ask them to "pay it forward." These people will each help three more people in whatever way they can. If each person helps three others every day for two weeks straight, 4,782,969 people will benefit from the original act of giving of just one person.

This movie inspired the creation of the Pay It Forward Foundation, which was established to educate and inspire young children, letting them know that they can change the world and providing them with opportunities to do so.

In this chapter, we'll describe the many different things you can give to others, including the following:

- love
- laughter
- knowledge
- leadership

- hope
- life
- time
- money
- skills
- health
- touch
- attention
- advice

love

True giving begins with love. Love is the most powerful force in the world, and when we love, we are in touch with our basic and most fundamental human need.

The great religions promote generosity and care for others. For example, Christianity says, "There are three things that will endure—faith, hope, and love—and the greatest of these is love" (in this verse, the word *charity* is often used instead of *love*). In Buddhism, one of the seven treasures practitioners must cultivate is generosity. In Judaism, *tzedakah*, or "charity," is the prescription to build a better world, and Jews are brought up to perform *mitzvahs,* or "good deeds." The Koran urges followers to help others and to give to people in need. In other faiths, such as Hinduism, generosity is lauded and perceived as a possible path to salvation.

Love is something all people need, no matter their background, culture, or faith. It is what makes all people, as Rumi says, "fellow travelers in the journey of life." Everyone—your spouse, friends, coworkers, neighbors, acquaintances—has the same need to be accepted and loved that you have.

Many people grow up in difficult circumstances, and almost everyone at one time or another has suffered emotional wounds, dashed hopes, or the loss of love. All people are complicated, and as they try to make their way in the world, sometimes they offend you, hurt you, ignore you, or lack compassion for you. You have probably caused the same emotional pain to others, sometimes unintentionally, sometimes not. This is why giving the gifts of compassion, understanding, and unconditional love is so important. It helps to break the negative cycle in relationships and leads to a revival of love and commitment because when people receive love, they learn to give love.

LOVE ISN'T ALWAYS EASY

A key part of love is willingness to give through sacrifice. Parents sacrifice many things to care for their children. Sleep comes to mind first, but if you are a parent, you could make a very long list. Love allows you to make these sacrifices. Having children, in fact, is the perfect example of the joy of giving. A form of giving is "giving up" pleasures or previously important priorities. (Did we mention you sleep less?) You choose new priorities based on your values and love.

In a healthy relationship, you love your spouse unconditionally—loving that person for who he or she is and not for who you want them to be. As you may know, this is not always an easy thing to do. And yet, what a gift it is, for both parties.

Adults have an easier time loving their children unconditionally (especially before they become teenagers) but have a harder

time loving other adults unconditionally. That's because unconditional love takes a great deal of time, commitment, compassion, and mindfulness.

Mindfulness means that you are conscious of your motivations, feelings, and thoughts, examining them regularly. You are
also willing to let go of outcomes, also known as nonattachment.
To achieve nonattachment, you must train your mind to understand that you can't control the outcome of all situations and
events. You can still care about, struggle to achieve, and hope for
a certain outcome, but whether you get what you want or not,
you realize it's still okay.

Of course, this is much easier said than done. Millions of
Buddhists and others struggle with this practice each day, sitting
in meditation to increase their mindfulness. For many people, it's
a foreign concept. And yet, increasing your mindfulness is a great
gift of love to yourself and to all those who come in contact with
you. It allows you to reduce tension, increase understanding, and
build strong relationships. After all, the better you know yourself,
the better a person you can become.

For example, try to apply mindfulness to a time when you are
angry. Anger is often a manifestation of another emotion, such
as fear or sadness. Being mindful of what's behind the anger can
help you heal yourself and love others better. Ideally, you will
develop the ability to explain your emotions in a sensitive way so
that instead of expressing anger, you can express your underlying
feeling, such as "I feel sad."

By figuring out the reasons you feel the way you do, and by
expressing your feelings in a kind manner, you deepen relationships. It's also a significant step in your personal growth. Mindfulness allows you to figure out what your feelings are, how best

to express them, and when to express them (or not). The best book we've seen on this subject is *Anger* by Buddhist teacher Thich Nhat Hanh. It will teach you to reduce your anger and to heal relationships.

WHAT LOVE IS NOT

The word *love* is often misused. How often have you heard someone say one of the following sentences?

> "He loves money."
> "She loves shoes."
> "They love to fight."

Almost every week you'll hear the word *love* used in ways that distort its real meaning and power.

Love of money is not love. Love of money may be an obsession, a compulsion, an emotional need—but it is not love. Love of shoes or other goods, likewise, is not love. It may be a lust for particular objects or possessions, but it is an illusion.

On their deathbeds, people do not say "If only I had had more shoes in my life." Their parting thoughts are usually about loved ones or the mistakes they made with their loved ones. There may also be other loves: their pets, nature, or their own contributions to the world—mostly gestures of sacrifice and love. Their regrets will often center on lack of love or sadness for relationships that went wrong. Frequently in their final days or moments they reach out to do what they could not do while healthy—to resolve the great pain caused by lack of understanding, lack of compassion, and lack of love.

In *The 7 Habits of Highly Effective People*, Stephen R. Covey reminds us that "love is a verb." It's not passive. It requires practice and action. Has your concept of love been warped by the Hollywood and television interpretation of love? Movie love happens fast, is fleeting, and is often cruel and shallow. In the real world, love needs time to develop and time to solidify. When you give love, you receive love. Real love is an example of how giving and receiving are so intertwined.

MAKING TIME FOR LOVE

Every week, we (Azim and Harvey) have private time with our wives, Farzana and Marcia. We go out for dinner, to the theater or a movie, to the gym, etc. One of our favorite outings is a long walk. It's wonderful.

The key to a successful date is having time to talk, to touch, to notice the changes in the other person, to articulate your thoughts and feelings. If you are financially strapped, you can always start, or join, a babysitting co-op. But do try to work private time into your own relationship. Believe us—you'll both love it!

These are among the most important hours in any week. You are giving attention, time, and focus to one of the most important relationships in your life. You and your partner will each benefit separately and also together.

Especially after they have children, couples need time to nurture their own relationship, so it is critical to protect one-on-one time with your spouse. Just think back to the pre-children days. You probably had lots of time with your loved one: time to talk, walk, make love, dream, and do projects together. But after children arrive, a couple's ability to spend quality one-on-one time is reduced by 90 percent. This is not exactly what you signed on for. Devoting special time to a relationship, when you are not both exhausted, is critical. It's also one of the best things you can do for your children. They want their parents to be happy and to stay together.

EXPRESSING LOVE

True love is selfless. It is free and liberated. It encourages change and growth. Love is timeless, and deep love continues to live even after our death. Love that is not expressed, however, does not reach its fullest potential because the more one expresses love, the deeper it becomes.

We do recognize that giving love often takes effort. How many people think they are too busy with their own lives to give time and love to others? How many really support the people close to them? Support means encouragement. It means unconditional love. It means letting go of your plans for how you think their life should go and accepting them for what they themselves want to do with their lives. This is one of the greatest gifts that you can give to the people close to you.

Forgiving people for past mistakes and hurts is also a way to express love, and forgiveness is a wonderful thing to give. Like you, other people are only imperfect humans. Keeping hurt and anger in your life is often an excuse to avoid getting close to people for fear they will hurt you again. People want to know that they are special in your life and that you care about them. If fear is keeping you from loving them—if, for example, there is a conversation that you want to have with someone but are afraid to—our advice is to express it: have the conversation anyway, in spite of your fear! Sometimes you just have to take a risk; such risk taking can be a sincere form of love.

For example, Michelle did not like the way her mother was always putting pressure on her to get married. She especially didn't like it when her mom did this in front of relatives and guests. That really hurt Michelle. She was thirty-seven and wanted to get married, and the last thing she needed was embarrassment and pressure. Michelle finally confronted her mother in a "private chat." She told her mom that she really wanted to get married, just as much as her mom wanted her to. However, Michelle warned her mother that when she brought up this issue in front of other people, she was making Michelle ever more resistant to the idea of marriage. Michelle told her mother that she would be happy to discuss this one-on-one with her, but that her mother should stop bringing it up in front of other people. Michelle's mother was relieved to know that her daughter was seriously looking for a partner, and she did not want to rock the boat. Things got better after the talk, even though there were occasional lapses. After all, it is Mom we are talking about!

Finally, never procrastinate when it comes to offering love. Not long ago, Azim attended the funeral of Ronale Sanjay Naidu, a friend's twenty-one-year-old son. It was a remarkable experience seeing how deeply everyone was affected by the loss of a talented young man. The parents' grief was deep and painful. Azim vividly remembers the cries of pain from the father and the mother as they came out of the cremation ceremony for their son. The family members and friends of the departed child knelt for hours, dumbfounded and grieving the loss of such a young man. There was a sense of utter loss all around, yet at the same time there was unity in response to the great loss. Everyone was united in the grieving, and everyone wanted each other's support. Each gave to the other whatever comfort they could in this very difficult circumstance. It is good to have this kind of giving, love, and support at such a time, but it should not be saved only for the death of a loved one. Give all the love you can to your family and friends while they are still alive, and tell them often that you love them.

laughter

Laughter is a sign of life. It creates happiness. It helps people cope with grief, aids creativity, and eliminates boundaries. It makes hard things easier. When we share our joy, our joys multiply; when we share our sorrow, our sorrows diminish.

Our lives today are pummeled by everything from economic difficulties to war and health pandemics. Everyone needs some laughter to ease the stress of these and other problems.

Like many clichés, "Laughter is the best medicine" contains a lot of truth. Scientists have long known that when you laugh, your brain releases powerful chemicals called endorphins. Endorphins ease pain, increase alertness, and literally bring you the feeling of joy.

According to the LAUGHS Web site, a child laughs one hundred fifty times a day. An adult laughs only an average of fifteen times a day. When you consider that adults with children certainly laugh more than fifteen times a day, this may mean that many adults do not laugh at all. And that's not funny.

TRAGICALLY FUNNY?

Comedian Carol Burnett's definition of humor is "Tragedy plus time." Think about it. How many times have you looked back at a disaster in your life and laughed about it? Of course, you won't laugh at all the disasters, but many of them can indeed be funny if you search for their humorous aspect. The uncle who stands up at your wedding and says all the wrong things—funny at the time? Probably not. Funny a few years later when you are sharing wedding disaster stories with friends? You bet it is.

One of Harvey's personal goals in life is to narrow the gap between tragedy and laughter. When he and his wife, Marcia, find themselves in a disastrous situation, rather than wait a few months, they almost always laugh during the disaster. It helps.

And don't just laugh at yourself. Narrow that gap between tragedy and laughter and share your hilarious stories with others. They will get a laugh out of them and will possibly gain the encouragement they need to laugh more in their own lives.

Harvey remembers trying to distract his crying, fifteen-month-old baby, James, who was sitting in his high chair. In desperation, Harvey grabbed three grapefruits and started juggling. James stopped crying. Harvey put some "oomph" into the performance when he accidentally bounced a grapefruit off the ceiling. James started laughing out loud. So Harvey kept bouncing the fruit off the ceiling. Soon James was laughing so hard that tears were rolling down his face.

What a gift laughter can be. Physiologically, it relaxes you. Research shows that it helps you cope better with pain. Laughter and humor can defuse tense situations too. We can't count the number of times we've turned exhausted, cranky children into smiling, happy kids again by acting like a clown (slapstick seems to be universally appealing to kids). Anyone can give this gift of laughter to others.

People have long coped with sorrow by using humor. It offers a positive spin on a difficult situation. A few years ago, it appeared that Harvey had cancer. He called his staff together to tell them he had had three positive tumor markers and was going for a CT scan the next day. He felt the need to crack a few one-liners to reduce the tension, and it worked. Five minutes after the meeting, he popped his head into the office next door and deadpanned to his friend, "Hey, Allan, I've got cancer, so could you get me a coffee?" Allan (and Harvey) found it hilarious. (Luckily, Harvey did not have cancer.)

In many cultures, humor is one of the best ways to cope with pain. All of us endure suffering in our life, no matter how wealthy or healthy we are. It ebbs and flows depending on our circumstances and the world around us. Laughter reduces the pain and fear. Indeed, some of the greatest humorists grew up in horrible conditions. Humor is a coping mechanism that is a gift for everyone.

The Buddhist Ram Dass tells the story of a man who asked a group at a workshop how they would feel when visiting a twenty-eight-year-old mother of four who was dying of cancer. The responses were predictable: sadness, anger, pity, horror, and confusion. He then asked, "How would you feel if you were that twenty-eight-year-old mother and everyone who came to visit you felt that way?" How much more would that woman appreciate a visitor who brought humor into her sickroom? Probably a great deal, given all the sad and gloomy visitors she had been receiving!

Harvey's mother died a slow death from cancer, spending six months in a hospital. Yet she probably laughed more in that time than in the previous six years. Harvey moved back from the West Coast to the East Coast for five months so he could support her and his father through this journey. The first few weeks were incredibly difficult. Then Harvey (and his sister, Moira, who also returned home) started taking a yoga/meditation class twice a week. From a state of constant exhaustion, both of them began to feel increased energy and lightness. Thanks mostly to this new energy and change in attitude, they enhanced their ability to make their mother laugh.

Harvey's entire family agrees that one of the highlights was Harvey's first attempt to cook a turkey. He didn't allow enough time for it to thaw, so it went in the pan half-frozen. Since it wasn't very flexible, he put it in upside down so it would fit. He managed to get the giblets out of one end. However, twenty-five minutes after Harvey put the bird in the oven, a friend asked if he got both the neck and giblets out. Harvey learned, to his surprise, that a turkey has two ends to empty. Thankfully, he managed to get the bag out before he poisoned his father. At the end of the cooking time, the turkey came out gray, with damp peeling skin and overcooked meat. It was a serious contender for the worst cooked turkey in history. Harvey's mother, who was a fabulous cook, was so entertained by the story that Harvey was delighted to have eaten a tasteless turkey just to see her laugh so hard.

We all have great stories—usually with ourselves as the butt of the joke—that can amuse, entertain, and enlighten. Use them as a gift.

Almost every night, Azim tucks his thirteen-year-old son into bed. Invariably, Tawfiq wants to hear funny stories before he goes to sleep, and he prefers unique and original tales. Azim combines philosophy with humor and starts most of his stories with the words "Gorgi Porgi did . . ." Gorgi Porgi has come to symbolize someone funny and hilarious to Tawfiq. By mixing philosophy with fun, Azim is able to pass on valuable lessons to his son in a lighthearted, humorous manner, while sharing quality time with him.

Laughter, like many qualities, has a potentially negative side. It can be used in a cruel way, to mock others, to discriminate, or to shame. Like any tool, it must be wielded carefully and with sensitivity in order for its wonder and power to be displayed.

How do you share the gift of laughter? Well, begin by asking yourself what makes people laugh. Jokes. Storytelling. Witticisms. Physical humor. Lots of things! Just figure out what makes you and your friends laugh, and get more of it. There are hundreds of funny Web sites, many hilarious books, lots of funny TV shows and movies. And, of course, funny people.

knowledge

Everyone (yes, everyone) has a story to tell, an experience that can help others. Your challenge is to extract these gems from your brain and your heart and, if you can, share them with others. When you share your knowledge with others, you break down barriers. You build openness and trust. By sharing knowledge, you become more valuable to your social networks and to the people you meet.

Both of us work with many nonprofits in many countries. We love training because it offers us the opportunity to pass on things we've learned. We are able to teach people ideas that work and warn them of ventures that will probably fail. That's also why we write books and record videos and CDs.

Both of us have benefited greatly from the wisdom others are willing to share. In fact, we've found that the smartest people we know are also the most sharing and generous. By sharing their wisdom, they, in turn, receive additional knowledge from others, thus showing that giving works both ways.

For the most part, news from any medium—from newspapers to television—gives you an awareness, although sometimes distorted, of reality. What it rarely does is give you a deep understanding of an issue. Books can give you a deeper understanding.

One of the things we both like to do is give books to people we care about. It's not always easy to find the right book because there are so many wonderful books that speak to the issues our friends are dealing with. Recently, however, there have been a few books that we've given to a number of people, including the following:

Seth Godin's *Survival Is Not Enough: Why Smart Companies Abandon Worry and Embrace Change* is an astute book about the speed of change in our society and how people can cope with it. We've given this (and other Godin books) to friends in fast-changing businesses.

Michele Borba, the author of *Building Moral Intelligence: The Seven Essential Virtues That Teach Kids to Do the Right Thing,* has great experience to share with parents. She offers many tips to help children survive and thrive in a very difficult world.

When the Body Says No: Understanding the Stress-Disease Connection, by Dr. Gabor Maté, is a beautifully written book about the mind-body connection, the impact stress has on our lives, and how we can help to protect ourselves from serious illness.

(It also shows that if you give "too much," it can have negative health consequences. Balance is the key.)

Do you have friends coping with the death of a loved one? We've given away many copies of Stephen and Ondrea Levine's *Who Dies? An Investigation of Conscious Living and Conscious Dying*, a powerful and healing book that has helped tens of thousands of people.

People appreciate receiving books that deal with issues relevant to their lives. And if you can't afford to buy a lot of books for your friends, you could just give them a synopsis of what you've learned so that, if they wish, they can buy their own copy or borrow it from the library. We sometimes send friends reviews from a Web site or a newspaper to let them know about a book that may be valuable and of interest to them—and to let them know that we are thinking about them.

Tim Sanders's book *Love Is the Killer App: How to Win Business and Influence Friends* contains an interesting chapter about the power of books and their importance to other people. Sanders is the chief solutions officer at Yahoo, and he spends a lot of time working with Fortune 500 executives. He uses his passion for books generously as a way to connect with other individuals. When he sees ideas in a book that may help people he knows or has just met, he shares the ideas with them and often buys them the book. Again, books (and knowledge) are a great gift to give people and a wonderful way to connect with them and to help them solve problems in their lives.

Sanders has also found that by sharing his learning, he benefits. We don't believe this is why he does it, but it is clear that he gains increased loyalty from other people. He helps solve their problems, and in turn they trust him as a confidant, a supporter of their work, and someone who cares.

TAKE AWAY THE TV

There are many ways to give by taking away. For example, if you spend too much time watching television, you can waste your life away. Yes, there are good television programs, programs that make you think, that inspire you and improve your life. But what percentage of TV programs fit that description? Groucho Marx once said, "TV is good for the mind; every time someone turns one on, I go into the next room and pick up a book."

Despite Groucho's gripe, television viewership continues to increase at an astounding rate. In 1998, for example, 70 percent of households in the United States received paid television services, which means dozens if not hundreds of channels. *Business 2.0* reports that by the end of 2003, the household percentage was up to 86 percent. The number of satellite subscribers doubled from 11.7 percent to 22 percent and is increasing rapidly.

In *Bowling Alone,* Robert Putnam describes how "heavy TV watchers reduce their civic involvement," if for no other reason than watching TV takes a lot of a person's spare time. This reduction in civic involvement impedes the building of stronger communities and healthier families, and it hurts giving in general.

We believe it's a gift to yourself and your children when you turn off your television. A friend did just that eight years ago when he saw that his three children wanted to spend all their time in front of the TV. He felt that it was bad for their health and bad for family life and that many of the values portrayed on the TV contradicted their family beliefs. He put the TV in the basement and cancelled the cable service. After a little adjustment, they were all happier. The kids got more exercise, the family played games together, and the kids became voracious readers. Recently, our friend's son, now fifteen years old, thanked his dad for this great gift. The son wasn't happy at the beginning, but he is very grateful now.

Try it. Your kids may be bored at first, but out of boredom comes creativity, interaction, and knowledge. They'll also have the time to volunteer for causes that will benefit them and others. If you think this is too drastic a step, you could restrict viewing to a set amount of time per day. Or, as another friend does, have one week on, one week off. And make sure that you are a good role model. If parents lounge for hours in front of the TV, restricting their children's access will understandably lead to resentment.

EDUCATION AND LIFELONG LEARNING

One of the best gifts you can give yourself and other people, especially children, is the love of learning. That's because changing circumstances can never remove this gift. When you are a role model—passionate about ideas, wisdom, and the importance of education—you teach their value. We believe the real purpose of education is to help people understand the meaning of life. According to the great teacher J. Krishnamurti, "[The] sole purpose of education [is] to help find out what you, with all your heart, must love to do!"

Education is much more than formal lectures and classes. Lifelong learning means you learn from your everyday experiences. Education may begin in the classroom, but it continues well after degrees and diplomas are bestowed. For most people, education lasts throughout their lives. Lifelong learning is what writer Conrad Squires calls "muscle building in the knowledge area, which is the bedrock for wisdom." And, of course, to succeed in the world today, to survive the rapidly changing work world, you need to continually improve your skills.

In his global travels, Azim speaks about lifelong learning as a key to success in terms of developing your full potential. He emphasizes that education is part of learning, but that learning encompasses much more. It includes the whole area of character building, of keeping an open mind, which allows you to respect other people, and of being humble, so that you understand that you don't know everything. This allows you to learn from every person, every encounter, every experience, and every difficulty.

INTELLIGENCE AND WISDOM

Those who are blessed with education and knowledge bear the responsibility of sharing their advantages with others. If we do not use these gifts we are given, we lose them. If we use these gifts to make a difference, we enhance them, increasing our knowledge and abilities.

All the great work of science, the exploration of creation, progress in medicine and health, developments in technology, communication, and travel, and the rise in the standard of living have been made possible through the use of intellect. All ideas and creativity are built upon the foundations of those who went before us. They gave us the tools, the teachings, and the skills to create and to pass on our creations to future generations.

Along with the fruits of your intellect, wisdom is a great gift to share with adults and children. Wisdom is a combination of knowledge, experience, and clarity. Some faith communities describe wisdom as the power of discernment. Ultimately, it is the knowledge of how to use your intelligence. When you share wisdom, you help people gain skills that allow them to learn on their own.

Both Azim and Harvey (and many people reading this book) had elderly relatives with limited education who were incredibly wise about many important aspects of life. For example, Harvey's uncle Russell never completed high school, yet he was a wise man, well read and active in the world. He also demonstrated incredible generosity and humor—gifts to all those who knew him. Azim's dad did not go to college, but he demonstrated his leadership qualities in business and volunteer organizations. He had gone to the University of Life, and he learned from his experience because he had an open mind. Look around you. You may find people in your family displaying similar wisdom, even if they do not have a higher education.

leadership

The concept of leadership means many things to many people. One person's strong leader is another person's dictator. People can be perceived as great and successful leaders in their work lives, yet their personal lives may be a shambles. True leadership, whether personal or corporate, makes a positive difference.

As people live, work, and raise families in the rapidly changing world of the twenty-first century, faced with financial insecurity and myriad stresses, they look for leadership to calm them in the midst of change, to tell them "Things will be all right," and to promise a happy ending. But leadership isn't that simple. Leaders who promise a simple panacea have too often brought repression and a denial of rights with their "easy" solutions. Research shows that people are more cynical than ever about leaders in all sectors of society.

One possible solution to this problem of leadership demands hard work, but it does bring results. It requires that you accept personal responsibility and give leadership yourself, guided by values not popularity.

You may scoff at this. You may think you can't be a leader. We believe you will be surprised at what you can accomplish once you've made a personal leadership commitment.

In his book *Leadership from Within,* Peter Urs Bender points out that every person possesses the seeds of greatness. It takes only two actions to become a leader:

- Develop the necessary skills.
- Overcome your greatest barrier—fear.

Bender believes most people "are afraid to stand out, to say what we feel, to risk being criticized, or look foolish. It is this fear that stops us from being the leaders we are looking for in this world." Becoming a leader can be frightening. It's more comfortable being a follower in a crowd. But while your risk may be less as a follower, so, too, are the rewards.

You can choose what leadership means to you. It may be volunteering to sit on the board of a community organization. It may mean being the first person to volunteer to raise money for a day care. It may even be having the courage to challenge ethical lapses in a business, government department, or a nonprofit.

A leader's value is in his or her ability to find the value of others. True leaders make a positive difference in the lives of people around them. They invite a shared vision so everyone contributes wholeheartedly to the success of the team.

The writer and teacher William Arthur Ward said, "A mediocre teacher tells, a good teacher explains, a superior teacher demonstrates, a great teacher inspires." The same is true for leaders. Effective leaders demonstrate many critical qualities:

- Leaders are solution oriented. They focus on solving problems, not on the obstacles.
- Leaders give by focusing on the important stuff, not the urgent stuff. They encourage others to focus on the important stuff too.
- Leaders take a long-term approach, so their giving is sustainable and they do not burn out.
- Leaders spend their time in building relationships. The most effective giving takes place when there is truth and respect.
- Leaders use their gut feelings and sixth sense to their advantage. They serve with love and compassion.
- Leaders create an enabling environment in which everyone is given a chance to mature to his or her full potential. They also create a fun environment.
- Strong leaders give. The corporate world uses the term *servant leader*. This may sound like a misnomer, but it is not. The best leaders are servants—wanting to serve and give.

Sounds like quite a job description, doesn't it? You can commit to building your leadership ability today. Work on your skills, and work on your fears.

CORPORATE LEADERSHIP

If you are a corporate leader, you may think it would be bad business to give away your corporation's time, money, and knowledge. One of the fundamental goals of a corporation is to make profits for its stockholders. Striving for profits is valid because corporate leaders work hard and take risks, and they need to be compensated for their efforts. These profits support their families and may be used for worthwhile causes.

However, no corporation thrives without giving to others. A business reaps profit and dividends in proportion to the service it gives to its customers, employees, shareholders, broader community, and the world. The better the service rendered, the greater the success or profits. When corporations take a collaborative approach and implement a "win-win" philosophy, they sustain their growth and success and provide critical leadership.

There is a worldwide movement to encourage corporations to implement socially conscious policies. As more and more consumers demand such policies, many business experts predict that corporations that show social responsibility will outpace their competition. Customers prefer to patronize companies that demonstrate they care about their workers and the environment and that generously support nonprofits. In a 1998 survey on social attitudes conducted by the Roper Center for Public Opinion, 65 percent of Americans said they were willing to switch brands and 61 percent said they were willing to switch retailers in favor of a company that was associated with a good cause.

The survey also found that 83 percent of those surveyed said they look more positively at companies that support a cause they care about. Among employees, 87 percent felt a strong sense of loyalty to their employer if the employer had cause-related programs, compared to a loyalty rate of 67 percent for companies that did not have a cause-related program.

How can you give? Bob Galvin, son of the man who founded mobile-communications giant Motorola, once remarked, "Dad looked down an assembly line of women employees and thought, 'They are all like my mom—they have kids, homes to take care of, people who need them.' " This realization motivated Galvin Senior to work hard to give his employees a better life. This is an example of corporate leadership.

When corporate leaders give of their time and wisdom to employees, they create new leaders in the team. When companies give extraordinary service and value to their customers, they retain the customers' trust and thus their long-term loyalty and business.

Some corporations fund creative microcredit programs in developing countries. These have helped poor people start businesses and remove themselves and their families from the cycle of poverty. This is an empowering form of giving in the corporate world.

Corporations rely on their good brand name for much of their value. If their brand value is destroyed by bad corporate practices, it will become known to investors, consumers, and communities where they operate. The information can be communicated to millions of people within minutes, thanks to the power of the Internet.

For many corporations, building brand value is tied to corporate responsibility. Giving back to their employees, the communities they work in, and the environment is key to corporate growth and survival in the future.

hope

Aga Khan IV said, "There are those who enter the world in such poverty that they are deprived of both the means and motivation to improve their lot. Unless they can be touched with the spark, which ignites the spirit of individual enterprise and determination, they will only sink into apathy, degradation and despair. It is for us who are more fortunate to provide that spark."

There are times in all people's lives when they need someone to believe in them—when they are feeling despair and a friend cheers them up or when, in the midst of impossible odds, they find the positive side of a situation. We all know that far too many teens missed the love and the care they needed as children. Many of them are in jail, on drugs, or struggling with painful memories.

Tina is a seventeen-year-old living in Tacoma, Washington. Two years ago she was addicted to alcohol and drugs, was living in a homeless shelter, and had already been arrested several times for assault. Tina grew up in a violent family where she wasn't given the love and care every child needs.

Then Tina was introduced to a group called Power of Hope. She went through a thirty-day drug rehabilitation program, and two years later she is still drug-free and has earned her high school equivalency diploma. She's following her dream to be a firefighter.

At Power of Hope, Tina regained hope—something that her hard life had beaten out of her. Power of Hope is a small group with a modest budget that does amazing things for teens in both the United States and Canada. When people help teens like Tina, they give those teens a chance to escape from the patterns of their past. This reduces crime and the financial costs of the judicial system. There are benefits all around.

For Tina or any person to reach his or her potential, hope is essential. If someone goes without hope for too long, it becomes difficult to even get out of bed in the morning.

To give hope to others, you must have hope yourself. Imagine you are not hopeful about your marital relationship, your children, your future, and your abilities. Imagine you have a goal or a dream but no hope. You will see problems instead of opportunities. You will cease to give because you feel "needy." You will be lost in the past and unwilling to move forward because you have forgotten that the past does not equal the future. The Sufis have a humorous way of describing this state: "You have been burnt with the soup and are now blowing at the yogurt!"

Kindness, mentoring, and listening are all ways to help give hope to people who have lost hope.

life

People have the power to save lives. You have probably heard of heroic feats that saved the lives of others: the dad drowning while saving his daughter's life; the mother jumping in front of a car to protect her son. Most lifesaving is less heroic but just as important. It could be counseling a friend who is suicidal or working on a crisis line, talking to suicidal people you will never meet. It could be donating blood. It could be becoming an organ donor.

Michael Nicoll Yahgulanaas's sister, Shelly, had a rare form of lupus. She had to get a kidney from a family member or else she would die. Michael, who is a well-known Haida artist living in British Columbia, gave her one of his kidneys and spent a year recovering from the surgery. His decision to donate a kidney was spontaneous. It didn't require thought or careful evaluation. It was a gift for Michael to be able to offer his kidney—a great feeling he would always remember as he sees his sister alive, rescued from imminent death.

Michael is one of a growing number of living donors who donate organs to loved ones or even to total strangers who share their blood type. Robert Putnam documented another powerful story in his book *Bowling Alone*. John Lambert was a sixty-four-year-old retired employee of the University of Michigan who had been on a kidney transplant waiting list for three years. Andy Boschma, a thirty-three-year-old accountant, heard of Lambert's situation and volunteered to donate a kidney. In addition to their generational and professional differences, Boschma was white, Lambert African American. They knew each other only through their bowling league. Andy offered his kidney because he liked and respected John.

Now consider the case of Jenny Oad, a healthy woman in her thirties. She always thought she'd be willing to donate a kidney if the situation presented itself. After a good friend committed suicide, she "felt a new empathy for people who are losing their loved ones well before their time." She decided not to wait.

Jenny found the Web site livingdonorsonline.org and read a post by Mike Fogelman, a fifty-two-year-old father of one and an advocate for children. They met and she offered him a kidney. The operation was a success, and Mike was given a new lease on life. Jenny's remaining kidney is working well, and she doesn't regret saving a stranger's life.

In the United States alone, 55,000 people are on the kidney transplant waiting list, and one in six dies before a donor is found. We are not suggesting that in order to be a giver you have to give an organ to somebody you don't know. In fact, since the U.S.-based United Network for Organ Sharing started keeping statistics in 1988, only 133 of the 46,241 kidneys taken from living donors were given to people the donors didn't know. Nevertheless, it's an incredible gift—a gift of life.

Many people pledge to donate their organs for transplants or medical research after they die. If your faith allows it, we encourage you to make this generous gift.

time

Time is your most precious commodity. Mismanage your time and you won't reach your potential. You might even cause serious family, career, or spiritual problems. Because your time is limited, when you give some of your time to others, you give a great gift. You are giving part of your life to someone or some cause.

Recently, an old man from Azim's community approached him and shared his personal grief. The man had been feeling guilty because of his actions over the previous ten years. Azim walked him through his actions and convinced him that what he had done was not as bad as he thought it was. A month later the old man rushed up to Azim and could not stop thanking him for making him see reality clearly. It had taken Azim only ten minutes of his time. Small investments of time can make a big difference.

Managing your time well allows you to find the time to give or to give more. With every passing second, you choose how you spend your time. You may think, "I have to go to work," "I must clean this room," or "I need to eat my dinner," but though these activities may be important, you need to be conscious that you are choosing to spend your time doing them and not something else.

You may choose actions because you want to avoid the consequences: getting fired, betraying a commitment, or going hungry. You may choose to do things because you are unable to resist external or self-inflicted pressure or temptation. But the key is to remember that you have a choice.

A great way to remind yourself of the value of time is to take each moment as if you've been reprieved from death and given a new lease on life. How would you spend your time?

Azim has a habit of budgeting his weekly time between family and work. He also keeps track of where he spends his time. (In his book *Seven Steps to Lasting Happiness,* he shares his time-budgeting process.) By allocating time to his family, Azim makes sure that he does not get so busy that he neglects his wife and children. By reflecting on the quality of this interaction and writing about it in his journal afterward, Azim confirms that this family time is not just "time tokens" that he has to spend but actually includes deeply meaningful interaction and bonding. He feels this is a great gift to give to his family, as well as to himself.

The exercise "How Are You Spending Your Time?" will help you examine how you manage your time.

how are you spending your time?

Ask yourself the following questions about time:

- Am I spending my time wisely?
- How much of my daily time goes to insignificant activities?
- What is the one regret I might have when I run out of time and depart from this world? Take some time to ensure that this regret will not manifest itself.
- If I do value each second, how will my day change?

The following actions can significantly improve your life:

- For fifteen minutes every day, spend time doing the most important thing in your life.
- For at least one hour today, spend time with the most important people in your life.
- Tomorrow, try to allocate your time so that it brings more balance to your life.

money

You choose how you spend your time every day; you also choose what you do with your money. Money is obviously a great thing to give, but if you are going to be a healthy giver of money, you will need to examine your feelings about it. And in order to have more to share, you will need to develop skills to manage your money more wisely.

WHAT ARE YOUR ATTITUDES TO MONEY?

You likely have a complex set of emotions attached to money, emotions that drive many of your life decisions—where you work, what you do with your money, and even if your marriage will survive.

The first time Harvey led a workshop on attitudes to money, he decided at the last minute to begin with a short meditation. He asked people to close their eyes, relax, breathe deeply, and clear their minds. After two minutes he asked them to think back to when they were young, to remember their first memory of money and the feelings attached to it. Since Harvey had his eyes open, he could see people visibly twitching. He asked them to remember those past feelings and then to bring their attention back to the present. He asked them to remember a recent money interaction that was emotionally charged and to recall those feelings. The twitching increased. People no longer appeared relaxed.

Harvey asked the audience to open their eyes and tell the group about their earliest memory of money. For the next twenty minutes Harvey could see people's emotions, buried for decades, rising to consciousness. These people—like most of us—had unresolved feelings around money. These feelings are always present, potentially sabotaging you and your pursuit of a fulfilling life.

The economic situations of the people in that room ranged from very modest to significantly wealthy. Every one of them had a money-related trauma. A fifty-year-old man describing his first memory of money imitated his wealthy dad's voice saying "Money doesn't grow on trees." One woman said, "We were always told we had no money for things I wanted."

The range of memories was startling. Everyone's attitudes were affected at an early age.

How about you? Did you have a lot of money while noticing that other people lacked money? Did you resent people who were rich? Did one or both of your parents frequently waste money on goods they never used? Were people fighting over money in your family?

Money produces strong emotions: fear, anger, envy, and greed. It is good to examine your attitudes to money so that you can avoid passing on to your children your complicated and often destructive emotions about money. Try doing the exercise "How Do You Feel About Money?" It may help you discover your attitude to money.

how do you feel about money?

Find a quiet space where you can relax. Breathe deeply so that your body and mind are calm. Wait until you are relaxed, then cast your mind back to your childhood or teen years and remember an emotional exchange around money. What do you remember? What do you feel? What lessons have you absorbed, if any?

Don't try to judge these feelings or other people's actions. Simply try to describe the emotions, yours and others', and what impact they might have had on you.

Now put yourself into a relaxed state again. This time, think of a recent interaction where you and another person had a highly emotional discussion centered on money. Then ask the same questions: What do you remember? What do you feel? What lessons have you absorbed?

This will help you identify some of your money issues and triggers. It's only after discovering these underlying issues that you can deal with them to reduce negative imprints on your life.

Conflict around money is said to be the number one cause of divorce in North America. When we examine our attitudes to money, we can help ourselves have more peaceful relationships with our spouses as well as with others.

If you have "money issues" you'd like to work out, Lynne Twist's fine book *The Soul of Money* is an excellent tool to help you.

DO YOU KNOW THE DIFFERENCE BETWEEN "WANT" AND "NEED"?

If you ever catch yourself saying, "I need a new _____," stop yourself. Most people in the Western world confuse want with need. You may want a new car, new shirt, or the newest electronic gizmo, but ask yourself, "Do I actually need it?" The second question you must ask is, "What am I giving up in order to obtain it?"

In many wealthy Western societies, a majority of people are in debt. The number of bankruptcies is rising, and credit card debt, with exorbitant interest rates, is rapidly escalating. People are sinking into a debt pit because they believe that possessions will assuage the hurt in their soul. Meanwhile, the consequence of this debt, this "need to acquire," is more pain. Trying to stay on top of their debts, people stay in jobs they hate or they abandon jobs and colleagues they love in search of more money.

Obviously, a basic level of money and possessions can simplify your life, reduce your stress, and help you achieve your goals, but too many people seem to believe making money and owning possessions are the main priorities in life, in spite of evidence to the contrary.

Do you know a wealthy person who is depressed? Or people who seem to have all the newest gadgets but have horrible relationships with their spouses? Or a middle-aged millionaire suffering from a debilitating disease?

Many people would trade their wealth in one second for true love, happy children, good health, or freedom from depression. When they honestly think about their priorities, money and "things" are often not at the top of the list. Once a person has financial comfort, in fact, money drops far down the priority scale.

So, is money bad?

No, money is neither bad nor good. Like water or fire, money is powerful but neutral. Your body needs water to live, but water can also drown you. Fire can keep you warm, but it can also burn you. The same goes for money. It is often used for good (feeding your family, protecting others), but it can also be used for evil (as a means of control or an object of unhealthy obsession). Money can be a form of energy. When you share it generously, you get more energy back, often in different and more valuable forms.

When you don't share it, you block that flow of energy, and this blockage can cause problems.

Each of our spending choices can make a difference. For instance, when you buy organic foods, as opposed to food sprayed with pesticide or injected with antibiotics, you help protect the environment. Similarly, you can choose to invest in tobacco companies that contribute to thousands of deaths each day, or you can invest in companies that have a social conscience.

When you can consciously determine the difference between wants and needs, you'll likely have more to give.

MANAGING MONEY

One of the most lasting and valuable gifts you can give yourself is money-management skills, or financial literacy, part of which is learning how to give. The measure of financial wisdom is not how much you make but how much you keep, how much you give, and how you manage your money. If you spend your money wisely, you can achieve many great things, for yourself, your family, and your community.

Giving money to other people can also accomplish much. Giving money to local, national, or international organizations can help those groups do many things. It can help them provide shelter and training for homeless or unemployed people; save and preserve endangered habitat and wild species; search for a cure for a devastating disease; support writers, musicians, or artists as they create new work.

Azim's friend Hussain Tejany heads the First Micro Finance Bank Ltd in Pakistan. Its role is to lend money to poor individuals and families so that they can start a small business. The idea is that if these people have a small business, they will be able to support their families, preserve their dignity, and not be a burden to the country or anyone else. This way, in the end, everyone wins. In the short time that the organization has been in existence, it has achieved phenomenal success. To date, the bank has lent around $10 million (U.S. dollars). The loan repayment statistics are high—over 98 percent—and the success rate of these businesses is also high. The keys to this model are empowerment, training, and the belief that human beings have the capacity to succeed. What a great gift to give!

skills

Everybody has something that they can do better or more easily than other people, some talent or skill they were born with or that they have developed. Your skill is another thing that you can give, either by using it to help an individual or a group or by teaching it to others.

We both know that, since we were children, we have constantly learned from others—from our peers and from adults. Each interaction with others, each new experience, enhanced our knowledge. Sometimes we learned new lessons, sometimes not. Because we know we've learned so much from others, we believe that passing on our skills is a gift to repay those who taught us so much.

Sharing skills also gives back to you. The more you share your skills with others, the more you enhance them. You might also learn new skills.

SHARING SKILLS

You might think you have no skills to share, but there is always something you enjoy doing or that you are good at that could benefit others. For example:

- If you are a good soccer player, you can offer to coach your child's soccer team. This gives you a chance to bond with your child and also to make a contribution to the community around you.
- If you have accounting skills, you can help a non-profit organization learn how to keep its books and accounts, as well as help it complete tax returns.
- If you have strong communication skills, you can help a social service agency by volunteering to handle calls from people having difficulty.
- If you have leadership skills, you can volunteer to be a board member for a nonprofit.
- If you have skills in any field, you might donate your services to people or organizations who are unable to afford your services. Johanna Vondeling, a professional editor who helped us with the structure of this book, told us: "Reading the [manuscript] . . . actually inspired me to do something I had been thinking about for a long time: training to become a literacy tutor. I'm now almost done with my training, and I'm looking forward to meeting my first student. I'm very excited about it." Johanna has wonderful skills and the desire to help; she just needed a little motivation (and we are thrilled it was this book that

gave it to her). Both she and the students she will help
will benefit from her kindness and skills.

There are so many ways you can share your skills. Both of
us have been involved in many boards, organizations, and communities in voluntary leadership capacities. Our involvement has
been mutually beneficial since we have contributed to these
causes and have indirectly received something back from them.
The benefits have ranged from learning new skills and learning
from the experience of others to building new networks.

The rewards that come from your involvement are not the reason
for your contribution. However, when you give unconditionally, the
power of giving kicks in—you end up receiving as much as you gave, if
not more. Sometimes the rewards are tangible, as when you learn new
skills or build your network. Sometimes they are intangible, as when
you gain inner satisfaction and happiness from your contribution.

BUILDING SKILLS TO GIVE

Recently, Harvey was at a beach party with a number of families. He
was fascinated watching the children, aged four to eight, who decided
to start a construction project with driftwood. They collected the
wood, negotiated responsibilities, designed the structures and sculp-
tures, and worked cooperatively and enthusiastically. It occurred to
Harvey that if all adults worked with this level of passion, focus, and
creativity, the world would be a different and much better place.

But what really struck Harvey was the realization that the children were developing many skills, including the ability to work
with others, learn from others, share knowledge with the younger
children, delegate and accept responsibility, and be creative. The

result was a marvelous little forest of creativity, built by proud and happy children, and admired by their delighted parents.

Children, as this example illustrates, develop their life skills best by playing. Adults too often forget how they acquired many of their skills and believe that once they pass a certain age, they are "too old" to learn anything new.

Regardless of your age, each day you have an opportunity to enhance your skills. And this can include your skills for giving wisely. "What New Skills Do You Want to Develop?" is an exercise that might help you identify a new skill you want to learn.

what new skills do you want to develop?

To develop new skills, ask yourself:

- What am I most passionate about?
- What skills could I learn in order to be able to pursue these passions?
- How can I acquire these skills?
- What support will I need?
- Will I be able to ask for this support?
- Will I commit to learning these skills today—right now?

If your answer to the last question is "Yes," write a contract with yourself right now. Select the date when you will start, and choose who you will tell about your commitment.

There are so many skills you can learn that will help you give to others. Here are a few highly valued skills:

- The ability to communicate effectively. Communication takes many forms: writing, speaking, and, perhaps above all, listening. These skills make it easier for you to give the gifts of compassion, understanding, and happiness.
- The ability to take full responsibility for your attitudes and reactions.
- The ability to read and to apply your learning in your daily life.
- The ability to deal with conflict in a positive and constructive manner.
- The ability to manage money so that you have enough for your family, yourself, and good causes.
- The ability to meditate and reflect in order to be self-aware. Self-awareness allows you to confront your weaknesses and recognize your emotions, which are crucial steps if you want to be more compassionate, understanding, and mindful. It can help you heal yourself and heal others.

If you want to make a difference in other people's lives, you simply have to find the right way to apply your talent, your skills, and your energy. And the more skills you develop, the more you can give.

health

One of the best gifts you can give to yourself and to those you love is the promotion of good health. Adopt healthy habits, eat healthy food, and maintain an active lifestyle. Teach your children healthy habits.

The human body is a complex mechanism, and quick-fix attitudes about health are just not good enough. Indeed, old age—which can be such a wonderful time of life—will be painful, even unbearable, if your health has deteriorated.

There are countless benefits of good health. When you are in sound health you sleep better, work better, serve better, feel better, think better.

touch

What gift can you give to children that will make them less aggressive and more understanding? Dr. Tiffany Field, a developmental psychologist and professor of pediatrics, believes it might be the simple gift of touch.

After observing preschool playgrounds and McDonald's restaurants in Paris and Miami, Dr. Field and her fellow researchers found that Parisian mothers touch their children more often than American moms do. They also discovered that the Parisian teens at McDonald's touch each other more often than their counterparts in the U.S. do. The American teens, in fact, were more likely to touch themselves (they would play with their hair, for example).

The other discovery the researchers made was that the French children were far less physically aggressive on the playground than the American children. Also, compared to their U.S. counterparts, French teens were much less verbally aggressive.

Statistics show that the level of violence among children in the United States is tragically high. Is lack of touch the only reason? Probably not. But people of all ages need to be touched, hugged, kissed, and loved. As Charlotte Diamond sings, "Four hugs a day, that's the minimum." Have you ever offered a hug to a person going through emotional pain? It helps. Have you ever kissed a child's injury? It helps too. Touch is a gift that everyone can give.

You may have heard about children in orphanages in Romania who were hardly ever picked up or touched. As they grow up, many of them cannot integrate into society. They will always have difficulty bonding with others, primarily because of the lack of physical and therefore emotional contact during their early years.

Try massaging a baby—infants like a massage just as much as you do. Harvey and his wife, Marcia, give their children brief massages before bed every night (their children have them well trained). When their son Ian was three, Marcia gave him a particularly long massage. Ian kept saying, "Do my feet, ears, toes, hands . . ." until almost every part of his body had been massaged. As Marcia kissed him good night and got up to leave, Ian said, "Hey, what about my thumbs?"

Dr. Field says, "We are establishing very clearly that touch is as important as diet and exercise in our children's healthy growth and development. I would like to see parents beginning to massage their babies right from the newborn nursery. We all need a daily dose of touch." She also reminds us that even adolescents love having their heads and backs rubbed.

Touch feels good to most people. You just have to remember that others feel the same way you do. And, of course, we emphasize that you should ask people if it's okay before you hug them.

attention

One of the best gifts you can give people is your respect, displayed through active listening. The Chinese philosophy is to listen with the eyes, ears, heart, and undivided attention.

Doctors know the best way to prescribe is first to diagnose, and the best way to diagnose is to listen. When you listen, you should not be preparing to respond because then you miss out on what is being said. Just listen carefully.

Recently, Azim did a presentation for a cancer group. He started his presentation by saying, "If I say to you I know and understand your pain, I will be lying to you. The truth is I don't. I do not have cancer and do not know how it feels to have cancer. So help me understand how you feel and what your biggest challenges are before I say anything to you."

The group responded by expressing thoughts like:

"Why me?"
"I feel a loss of control."
"I'm angry."
"I'm afraid."

These are real issues with no quick-fix solutions. Azim did his best to respond to them, but the fact that he actually took the time to ask the question and be attentive to the group's feelings

was important. The participants felt that their feelings were valued, so they responded favorably to Azim's presentation.

Giving people space to express how they feel and listening
attentively to them is a valuable form of giving. And when you
actually listen to people, you can give more appropriate and sensitive advice.

advice

All creatures give advice. A kangaroo teaches her baby how to
hop, how to hide, how to eat. She's giving advice so her joey will
survive and prosper and produce more baby kangaroos. All animals are programmed to give good advice to their young. Their
advice is designed to ensure the survival of their species. It's only
when rapid change occurs in an animal's environment that the
parents' lessons fail to protect their offspring.

When humans give advice and share feelings or opinions, it
can be a sign of concern and love. But it can also be perceived as
an attempt to control. Advice can be powerful, compassionate,
and life-enhancing, or it can be misguided, hurtful, and misin-
terpreted. Always ask if your advice is wanted. Often a listening
ear and an understanding mind are all that people want. When
you do give advice, spend one-third of your time talking and
two-thirds listening.

Almost all humans give advice, so it is good to learn better
ways to give and receive advice. No one is objective about the
reality around them. Everyone brings their unique experiences,
thoughts, and interests to any situation. By having others offer
their perspective, you can get a more balanced view, tap into a

vast array of experiences, and often make better and healthier decisions.

If you look back on your life, you can see particular people whose counsel to you has changed your life. Their advice has made a difference, perhaps in your career, the way you raise your children, the place you choose to live, or your choice of education. For their advice, you recognize these people as mentors, dear friends, or simply the people you love.

It's hard to be objective about the quality and usefulness of your own advice to others, so how do you judge advice given to you? First, you have to gauge the experience of the givers. Do they have special experience, knowledge, or understanding? In a noncynical way, examine their motivation and try to determine if theirs is the best advice for you.

Second, if you catch yourself saying "That's what I *should* do," you can pretty much guess that you will in fact *not do it*. Your subconscious or the part of your brain that does not want to change (whether to reduce your pain or increase your pleasure) is at work.

Have you ever noticed that you can give great advice to other people—advice that would help them reduce or eliminate serious problems, seize opportunities, deepen relationships if they followed it—but they usually neglect to implement your suggestions, even when they wholeheartedly agree, "Yes, that's a great suggestion. That's what I should do"?

Should is a qualifier that essentially says "I'm not going to do that, despite its being in my interest." Look at these *should* statements:

"I should end this relationship."
". . . read more."
". . . quit this job."

Then there is the *I should not* group:

"I know I shouldn't have this drink."
". . . spend this money."
". . . eat this extra dessert."

You'll notice that these *should* and *should not* statements are usually followed by the word *but*. When people use *but* in a statement, it is the sound of their inner voice debating an issue. When you use the word *but,* you negate the first part of a sentence. Have you ever heard someone say:

"I love you *but* . . ."
"You haven't put on much weight *but* . . ."
"I'd like to stop smoking *but* . . ."

When you say, "I love you *and*" (instead of *but*), you can deliver information that you believe needs to be said (advice). You are less likely to alienate your loved ones with this simple substitution. They will listen.

When you are giving advice on an emotional topic, you must be sensitive to the other person's vulnerabilities and particularities. The language you use—your body language, as well as the words you speak—is crucial. Always use such phrases as "I feel that . . ." instead of "You need to . . ." or "You should . . ." It helps others listen to what you are saying, and they'll be more likely to follow your advice. (Note: We are assuming that the advice being offered is good. Of course, this is not always the case. For example, if you don't live up to what you say, your advice will lack credibility. It would be like the alcoholic who tells his kids not to drink to excess—the advice is sound, but the source is less than credible.)

You can always improve your communication skills, which will help you take action on advice given to you, as well as give advice that others are more likely to follow. You'll also have more impact if you understand the sensitivities of others: their backgrounds, their cultural upbringing, and so on. There are many books and courses that outline, for instance, the difference between how men and women think and talk. Deborah Tannen's book *You Just Don't Understand: Women and Men in Conversation* is one such source. As well, in *The 7 Habits of Highly Effective People,* Stephen R. Covey outlines a clear path to better communication—one that will increase understanding, reduce conflict, and promote healing. It's powerful and effective.

The key to good advice is to understand the circumstances, motivations, and feelings of the person you are counseling. Then your advice is more likely to be received with appreciation.

giving what you need most

Recently, Azim and his wife, Farzana, became involved in helping a colleague with his book sales. They were both thrilled to do so. It reminded them of the days when Azim was starting his new career and had to sell his own books. They remembered the struggle and sometimes the humiliation when no one would show up for a book signing or no one would buy what they thought was a great book.

This experience taught Azim two valuable lessons. The first is that it is good to remember your roots so that you can appreciate your fruits. The second is that when you begin to give to others the things you want for yourself (in this case, book sales), you have really understood the power of giving!

balance

One of the biggest challenges people face in the twenty-first century is the task of balancing the body, mind, and soul. We believe that personal balance allows you to give in healthier ways. And, perhaps most important, finding balance means you don't give "too much" so that you feel exploited or taken advantage of.

If you deplete your resources by giving too much, you reduce your ability to give in the future. In many ways, this is even more critical when you give emotionally. If your inner goodness becomes exhausted, then you may not be capable of giving again for a long time. Balance is the key.

Your balance may be totally different from anyone else's. Ensure that your balance is based on your own personal circumstances. For instance, at times your life will be out of balance—when you start a new job, have a health setback, or have a baby. At those times, it is a good idea to evaluate your giving to ensure that you move toward more balance.

The goal is to strive for balance to the best of your ability amid the circumstances in which you find yourself. Perfect balance may never be possible. However, being conscious of the benefits of balance will help you get closer to it.

As you strive for balance, take into account your priorities. And in determining your priorities, think of the long term. Ask yourself what is the ultimate purpose of your existence and what do you hope to achieve in your life. Then work backward from those goals.

Sometimes it seems that some components of the balance equation work against each other. For example, the more time you spend on professional development, the less time you are able to spend with family. Finding balance is really a matter of juggling your career, family, health, spiritual growth, financial management, and other related activities. Setting your priorities, basing them on your long-term vision and goals and combining them with the proper time-management skills can lead you to a balanced and harmonious life.

You also need to balance the various forms of giving. Some forms are more useful or appropriate than others. The key is to evaluate what and how you can give with your personal vision and goals.

What can you give that will create the highest impact—your time, your money, your skills, your advice, your attention? Can you give something even when you're having a bad day, a bad week, or a bad year? We hope that by reading this chapter you'll be encouraged to give something no matter what your circumstances may be.

key points

Everyone can give something. Even if you can't give money or material objects, you can give time, knowledge, wisdom, skills, leadership, attention, touch, advice, hope, laughter, or love.

Love is a universal need and spans all countries, cultures, and faiths.

Those who are blessed with knowledge and wisdom have a responsibility to share their knowledge and wisdom.

Time and money are both valuable resources. Give as much as you can of them both.

If you give people skills, you empower them.

When you give an attentive ear, you are giving utmost respect.

Give what you need most in order to experience the real power of giving.

Take a balanced approach to life and to giving.

to whom should you give?

We hope that as you read chapter two, you realized you had more to give than you first thought. While you were pondering what resources you had and which skills you'd like to develop, you may also have started identifying people and causes you'd like to help. In this chapter we highlight where you might direct the time, money, knowledge, wisdom, skills, and love you are giving.

We illustrate that you can give

- to yourself,
- to your family,
- to the community,

- to nonprofit organizations, and
- to the planet

start with yourself

You may be familiar with the expression "Charity begins at home." Sadly, people often use it as an excuse not to give to the poorest of the world because there are poor people living in their own community. In some cases, people who want to spend their money only on themselves quote this proverb as an excuse to avoid giving at all.

We believe that "Charity begins at home" has a different meaning. In its pure form, charity equals love. The "at home" part means you begin with charity toward yourself. The statement becomes far more powerful when you understand it as "Love begins with you." When you are charitable with yourself, when you love yourself, then you are more capable of giving to others—and you are more capable of receiving.

Many people may find it difficult to receive, for a variety of reasons. We believe that every person has to learn to receive as well as to give. Azim's friend Joy, a singer, told him about her difficulty in receiving: "I now consider giving and receiving to be a complete action. To give without receiving, or vice versa, lacks integrity and wholeness. They are like two sides of the same coin. Yet I've found it difficult in my life to complete the cycle by receiving. As a singer, I would find it difficult to stand on stage and 'allow' the audience to give me their applause. I was uncomfortable and wanted to cut them off and scramble offstage."

She realized that the audience needed to give applause for

what they had received. So now she waits for them to finish their applause before she leaves the stage. "Some people find it terribly difficult to receive even a sweet, simple compliment. I tease my friend that a compliment sticks to her like an egg to Teflon! So, yes, giving and receiving is a complete, whole, loving transaction."

LISTENING TO YOUR INNER VOICE

How many times have you known in your own heart that you were taking the wrong path? One part of you was giving advice to yourself, yet another part wasn't listening or was arguing for the wrong path. In order to accept and love yourself, you must listen to your various inner voices. (Psychologists call these competing voices "self talk.") When you really listen to the voices, you become more self-aware and can make decisions based on your core values.

Azim encourages people to write a daily journal to develop a habit of self-reflection that will make them more attentive to their inner voices. Hindu and Buddhist teachings (among others) also provide tools for observing how your mind works. Mindfulness—the ability to observe your thought process and to hear your different inner voices—can help you limit mental suffering.

According to author Joan Borysenko, meditation is the key to "achieve awareness of the mind so that thinking could be a matter of choice rather than of habit." Meditation can be as simple as sitting still, relaxing in a quiet place, and feeling your abdomen rise and fall as you breathe in and out. Regardless of how it is done, meditation helps you reflect on your actions and make better choices in life. In the words of an unknown author, "Listening to your heart, finding out who you are, is not simple. It takes time for the chatter to quiet down. In the silence of 'not doing,' we begin to know what we feel. If we listen and hear what is being offered, then anything in life can be our guide. *Listen*."

Meditation, like other things of value in life, takes time, commitment, and practice. Scientific research shows that meditation can be an excellent way to relax, build your immune system, and improve your outlook on life.

GIVE YOURSELF A BREAK

Most of us know people who are much harder on themselves than they are on other people, even people they don't like. Harvey had a particularly hard time learning how to give himself a break. As a youth growing up in a conservative Catholic church, guilt became his middle name—and boy, that is hard to change!

In a famous documentary film series that started with *7UP* and continued with *14UP, 21UP,* etc., Michael Apted follows the lives of fourteen people living in England, starting when they were seven years old. He visits them every seven years to film another segment. For a shocking number of the individuals portrayed in the film, the future seemed to be determined by how they were at the age of seven. One night Harvey was discussing this series with friends and asked them what they had wanted to be when they were seven years old. Eve had wanted to be a writer, and Alan wanted to draw. She is now an author, and he is an architect.

When they asked Harvey what he wanted to be, he had to

think for a minute. Then it hit him, like a bolt of lightning. When he was seven, he wanted to be a martyr, to sacrifice his life for others. Guess what Harvey spent the next thirty-five years trying to do.

He had so much compassion for others that he forgot himself. But during the last decade or so, that has changed considerably. Harvey says, "Among the most profound words I've ever heard were those a friend said to me, 'Be gentle with yourself.'

"Sacrifice is not all bad," Harvey continues, "and if I could save either my wife or my children by laying down my life, I'd do it. Most of us would." But if you devote your life to unrestrained sacrifice, you can't love yourself. You forgo all your needs for others, and then your giving isn't especially effective. You can lose your spirit and wither emotionally. You have to be aware of the needs of others but not to the total exclusion of your own emotional and physical needs. Balance and mindfulness are the keys.

Taking care of yourself, both emotionally and physically, is a central part of loving yourself. If you are weak, you can't take care of others, and if you have little to give, you won't reach your full potential. That's why giving to yourself is a critical component in your ability to give to others. Indeed, too many people can't give what they'd like to because they aren't strong enough emotionally, spiritually, and physically. Meanwhile, others may give too much and deplete their resources, thereby lessening their ability to contribute over time. These people are like runners who neglect to pace themselves in a marathon. They have a short burst of speed and strength but cannot sustain the energy required for the long haul.

We believe that when you take care of yourself, you exhibit the same kindness you want to shower on others. Nurturing your health, your skills, and your relationships will in fact enhance your ability to help others.

LEARNING THE HARD WAY

Admitting a problem is the first step to correcting it. When you take steps to deal with a problem—whether it's an inability to give to yourself or accept giving from others, stress from work or family worries, unhealthy habits like drinking too much or smoking—you are giving to your loved ones and your community. You become a healthier person, and that benefits everyone. Some alcoholics, for example, can only recover once they admit their powerlessness. They must recognize—and public recognition helps—that this is a weakness they probably can't overcome without help from others. Admitting a weakness or problem is a crucial step, as it allows you to accept—and allows people to give you—compassion, healing, and understanding. A confession of weakness may also lead you to feel anger, confusion, and sadness, but these are only preconditions of positive change.

When Harvey was thirty-six, he was close to burnout. His mother had just died of cancer. He left a seventy-hour-per-week job he loved and had worked at for a decade. A turbulent relationship finally ended. Single, unemployed, exhausted, emotionally fragile, and three thousand miles from his father, whose health was declining, Harvey was, as he admits, a mess.

Harvey was in a critical situation a lot of people experience in life. He was a classic unhealthy giver. As a matter of survival, Harvey decided to become healthy in a number of ways. He finally understood that by taking care of himself, he would be able to continue giving to others. So he decided to work part-time for six months, to cut back on expenses, and to seek therapy to understand his role in his burnout. He's happy to say that fourteen years later he leads a balanced life, with meaningful work and a wonderful family. In retrospect, he sees that he had to first give to himself so that he would be better able to give to others. In other words, despite his good intentions, Harvey couldn't help others until he was first able to help himself.

The exercise "The First Step to Helping Yourself" will allow you to identify and start to address what you need to do to help yourself before helping others.

the first step to helping yourself

Think back to a time when you admitted a weakness to someone you cared for. What was that person's response? Did it help you change? Are you willing to take this risk again? If so, with whom?

Make a list of the areas in your life that are weak and the areas where you would like to be strong. Make another list of the areas that are strong in a negative sense and that you might like to weaken.

This is an excellent exercise because the first step to solving a problem is to identify it. Each of us has developed negative habits over a long period of time. The second step is to really commit to changing them. Give yourself the gift of improving your life.

giving to your family

Creating harmony in the family leads to harmony in the world—one family at a time. You first learn to give within your family. You express your love and affection in the family by giving of yourself. And then that act of charity, which has begun at home, extends to everyone you meet in the world outside your home.

Azim's grandfather moved from India to Africa, all on his own, at the age of fourteen. When he reached Africa in 1914, war broke out and he had to go into hiding. Forty years later, when Azim was born, his family lived in a house without any floors. Things eventually changed. By the time Azim's grandfather died in 1963, the family had turned their meager beginning into prosperity. Today Azim lives in a safe democratic country and is thriving in his new profession, traveling around the world, speaking to large audiences. If Azim's grandfather had not taken a risk to go to Africa and sacrifice his childhood to create a better future for his family, would Azim be where he is now?

As far back as he can remember, Azim saw his father give his time, his wealth, and his wisdom. He always gave with respect, dignity, and humility. His father never told him to give, but Azim ended up being a volunteer anyway because of what he saw his father doing. It is not what we tell our children that counts; it is what we do that they emulate.

If, like Azim, you were fortunate enough to grow up in a family that taught you well, it is natural for you to teach the same lessons and behave in the same ways with the family that now surrounds you.

Did you grow up in a "functional" family? If you did, you

are in the minority. Dysfunction is the norm, yet most people still love their parents, children, and siblings and wish they could love them more. We believe it's possible to love more, but like most things that are really important in life, it is not always easy. Things of value rarely are. Working through a conflict in a relationship is not easy, but when you do so, the benefits can be enormous.

Are you willing to make a healthy family your priority? Are you willing to give your love unconditionally? Are you willing to examine your role in creating conflict or pain? If you are, then you need to know that improving all these areas of your life begins with changing yourself—because you are the only person you can really change.

GIVING TO YOUR SPOUSE

The most important relationship you have is with your partner. A loving relationship is a great joy for you and an inspiration to others. Your partner is a best friend who is always there to listen to you, support you, and love you. But creating an ideal relationship takes hard work, time, and a particular set of skills. Our plea to you, then, is to make it a priority to set aside the time to develop, strengthen, and celebrate this special relationship with your partner. This will be one of the greatest gifts you can give to those you love, and also one of the greatest gifts you can give to yourself.

Dr. John Gottman is a leading marriage researcher. Among the many useful things he has discovered is a ratio that can dramatically help your marriage. If you say five positive things to your spouse for each negative one, you have a good chance of having a successful, lasting relationship. It's simple, but do you follow this advice? If you do, why not work to eliminate all negative comments?

In their book *Conscious Loving: The Journey to Co-Commitment*, Gay and Kathlyn Hendricks argue that the real skill in maintaining successful relationships is telling the "microscopic truth." They define this as speaking "the truth about your intense experience as you are experiencing it." An example would be: "When you said you weren't coming home from work, I felt empty inside and had a rush of thoughts like, 'I'm not worth coming home to.' I hate being alone. It's just like when I was a kid." Practice this microscopic honesty and you will feel its great healing power in your relationships, as well as within yourself.

What else can you give to a relationship to make it happier, stronger, and enduring? We suggest the following six points:

- Give yourself time with your spouse. Azim, for example, schedules weekly private time with his wife, Farzana, which keeps their communication channels open and their relationship strong. Harvey has a regular "date night" with his wife, Marcia. And both Azim and Harvey set a high priority on spending time with their children and spouses every day.

- Give compassion. Knowing your partner's story will allow you to better understand him or her, and understanding is the basis for compassion. Children's TV entertainer Fred Rogers (Mr. Rogers) carried a slip of paper in his wallet that read: "Once you know a person's story, then you can love anyone." That's why it's so important to know all the details of your partner's story. There is always a reason for every action a person takes, and understanding and compassion are keys to helping you and others reach a better level of understanding. This will deepen your love.

- Be honest. A relationship cannot be based on lies. People are afraid to share the truth and often find it difficult to do so. However, honesty is a core value in the deepest and strongest relationships.
- Give love every day, in everything you do. Kindness is an expression of love, care, and concern. Love is active, not passive, and you should express it often. Knowing the specific form of love that is important to the special people in your life is crucial. Is it physical affection, gifts, verbal praise, or something else?

The BBC aired a documentary a few years ago on happy couples in long-lasting relationships. One of the secrets of their success was that although couples fell "out of love," they did it at different times. That is to say, one partner's love waned a bit while the other's was strong. The strong love nursed the weakening love back to health. Active loving reduces the chance of love waning or, worse, love waning in both partners at the same time.

- Give friendship. Harvey's best friend is Marcia. Azim's best friend is Farzana. "What luck," we think, but we know that friendship is hard work that involves the allocation of time, energy, and mutual concern and compassion.
- Give in sometimes. Every relationship that succeeds requires some degree of compromise on both sides.

If one side gives or takes too much, it's like an unbalanced teeter-totter. One person stays on the ground while the other is left up in the air. And the person who has overly compromised may decide to get off the teeter-totter, destroying the game, the fun, and the relationship.

HEALING RELATIONSHIPS

If one of your important relationships with family, friends, or work colleagues is damaged, the resulting emotional turmoil can limit the energy you have for "giving" activities.

How many people do you know who are estranged from their children or their parents? Do you have friends or acquaintances who finally resolved their difficult relationships with a parent when that parent was dying? Wouldn't it have been better to resolve the relationship when there was still time to enjoy life with that parent?

The suffering in loveless families extends way beyond the parent and child. It will include grandparents, grandchildren, and others who care about these wounded human beings. Unhealthy families lead to unhealthy communities and to an unhealthy world. We can start healing our world by first working on ourselves, developing our gifts of compassion, mindfulness, and commitment to positive action.

If you are estranged from a parent, relative, or friend, think of the joy that could be yours if you patched up your differences with that person. Think of the pain in your heart and in the heart of the estranged person that you could eliminate. Will you resolve to work on healing this pain? You may feel that the other party should take some responsibility, but someone has to take the first risk and maybe the second and third. It takes courage to show love, but it is worth the effort and risk.

One thing you can do for yourself and the other person is to give some thought to why the relationship is having problems. Fixing it is a gift you can give to yourself, your family (who suffer if you are having problems), and to the person whose relationship is damaged. Here are nine steps to healing a damaged relationship:

- Make a commitment to improve it.
- Visualize how it will be different.
- Recognize that it may take time, and be persistent. You must take the initiative.
- Recognize that you have to change first. You have to be open to the other person's position and feelings and accept that you may have to change your perspective and feelings.
- Don't look for solutions; look for emotions. Solutions can come later. Don't use accusatory language, such as "You did this." Use "I feel" language. If you feel angry all the time, go back to our first step.
- Don't deny that you have been hurt, sad, or angry. These are legitimate feelings. They are yours. You own them. You can keep them on display in your kitchen, you can store them in the attic, or you can just let them go. The choice is yours. When you name your feelings and share them with another, you have the power to finally let them go. However, counselor Carol Ann Fried has a warning about expressing

feelings. She says that it's not enough just to use the word *feel*. When you follow the word *feel* with the word *that*, it changes from a feeling into a thought. Her example, "I feel that this job is rotten," means I think this job is rotten. To make it a feeling, you must use a feeling word after feel. The four core feeling words are: mad, sad, glad, and scared. Thus, to express your feelings about a job, you might want to say: "I feel angry and frustrated at work. I really dislike my job!"

- Pray or meditate on the issues. This should help bring you calmness and perhaps even clarity.

- When you have a discussion, follow author Stephen Covey's advice: "Seek first to understand, then to be understood." It's hard to describe how powerful this is, but we assure you it will change the way you engage in every potentially divisive discussion.

- Be willing to be wrong. Should you compromise your values? No. But neither should you believe that your values—as determined by your upbringing—are the only legitimate ones. People may have different and equally valid values. Remember that your genes, environment, experiences, and society in general have all shaped your perspective. Not everyone has had the same background and social milieu, so not everyone sees things the same way. Be open to other experiences and viewpoints and to the way they affect the other person's perception of the problem. Remember that the problem is secondary to the relationship.

The exercise "How Healthy Are Your Relationships?" sets out some questions for you to ponder about your family and other relationships.

how healthy are your relationships?

Ask yourself:

- How healthy are my family relationships? Do they need to be healed? Are there unresolved issues? Buried pain?
- Am I willing to make my family my priority? Am I willing to give my love unconditionally? Am I willing to acknowledge my role in holding on to "toxins" that hurt me as much as my kin?
- What can change if I begin to give more within my family? What can I give to my family that requires a little effort but brings great results? What can I give to myself that will make me a happier and healthier person?

GIVING TO YOUR CHILDREN

Sahar, Azim's daughter, stopped playing soccer for a few years. When she rejoined the team with her friends, despite their best efforts they were losing every week.

Much to everyone's surprise, Sahar kept her head up and continued playing with enthusiasm and vigor. At first it was difficult to figure out where this superb confidence was coming from. As it turned out, Azim and his son, Tawfiq, had become Sahar's greatest cheerleaders. Both of them showed up for most of her games and her practices too. Their support boosted Sahar's confidence and also helped strengthen the relationship between Azim and his children and between the children themselves.

When you give time to your children, you strengthen your bond with them and enhance their esteem. Children, like adults, want to belong. They need to feel that they are important. Giving time and making sure your children are involved in your life will ensure that they feel they belong.

Our first gift to our children was the gift of life, and the giving never stops. We give love, time, attention, money, values, spirituality, networks, and more money! In return, they give us both pain and joy. We'd rather avoid the pain, of course, and some of us have more than our share of it, but don't forget that pain can make the joy ever more intense and beautiful.

Don't try to talk your children out of their feelings. Instead, allow them to express their feelings without fear of repercussions or ridicule. And don't punish your children for their feelings— even their anger. They need to learn that you love them even when they feel anger, which is a normal emotion. Let them know that you think their feelings and ideas—all of them—are worth sharing. They will learn to respect themselves and others because you have given them this important gift.

Here are a few suggestions to help build your relationship with your children:

- Get down to your child's level so you are not towering above him or her. Look a child in the eye.
- Teach your children to always tell the truth by practicing truth-telling yourself. Being a role model for

truth-telling might be one of your greatest gifts to your children.

- Reflect your child's feelings back to them when they offer them. "So you feel . . ." This is a sign of respect and also confirms that you understand what they are trying to communicate.
- Have frequent family meetings to discuss issues that are important to each family member. We know children who really open up about what is happening in their lives. If this exercise starts when they are young, they'll be more likely to remain "open" during their teenage years.
- Give your children lots of nighttime cuddles.

TEACHING GIVING TO YOUR CHILDREN

In his wonderful book *Soul of a Citizen: Living with Conviction in a Cynical Time*, Paul Loeb writes that children who teach younger children, write letters to people in the hospital, or make toys for poor kids are much more open to helping people in need when they grow up than those who don't share such experiences. It's no surprise. Children who are taught to care become caring adults. We believe adults must make a special commitment to teach children compassion through stories, actions, and mentoring.

Actions are a powerful teacher. One day when Harvey was out of town, Marcia and their children decided to go for a bicycle ride. As they were getting the bikes out of the basement, a stranger climbed out of the kids' backyard tree house.

Shocked, and protective of the children, Marcia yelled at him to get out of the yard, which he did. When he was on the other side of the fence, he said he was sorry he had to spend the night in the tree house. He had nowhere else to go. After listening to the man's story, overflowing with compassion (after all, she did marry Harvey), Marcia gave the stranger bus fare and fed him breakfast.

Beyond Marcia's good feelings for helping the stranger, and the man's gratitude for being shown some kindness, we think it was a good lesson for Harvey and Marcia's children. They saw that giving to others is the right thing to do. They saw their mother try to alleviate a stranger's suffering.

Every day, in many ways, you have the ability to develop a culture of giving in your home, one that can be a lifelong gift to your children. Giving your children an allowance is a good way to foster giving. Consider getting them to break their allowance into three portions, say 80 percent for spending, 10 percent for saving, and 10 percent for giving. The percentages can vary, but allocating their allowance to these three areas will help teach money-management skills to your children. This is an incredibly valuable gift.

We recommend that you allow your children to decide where they want to give their "giving" money, even if you disagree with their choice. Giving them the decision empowers them, and it gives them a strong emotional connection to their philanthropic gift.

You can reinforce their giving by telling them how much it means to you, as well as to those who were helped. Telling children about your own giving and how you feel about sharing what you have is great role-modeling. You will pass on your tradition of giving to them, and as they grow, they'll see that the gift of giving also gives back. They will likely pass it on to their children too.

By encouraging your children to give, you help them engage in civic life. That strengthens democracy and fights the cynicism so pervasive in our society—especially in the media. You will also teach children to care for other people, even people they may never meet, and to care for animals and nature.

Giving in its many forms helps develop understanding and compassion in children and reinforces their desire to learn much more about an issue that touches them emotionally. This might lead to their developing many useful skills, such as research, writing, and an understanding of their values and motivations.

Harvey remembers collecting money for poor people in the developing world when he was in the third grade. This could have been the reason he later worked for twelve years in the international development field, which gave him great inspiration, satisfaction, and understanding. We never know how our childhood experiences will affect our lives. When we help our children have positive experiences of generosity, we may be setting them on a path where they blossom as compassionate and fulfilled individuals. Some other ways to teach your children giving include the following actions:

- Model generosity to friends and strangers.
- Participate in community organizations and tell your children why you think this is important.
- Discuss responsibility and the golden rule with your children.
- Ask them to set aside 10 percent of their allowance for giving. Then match their gift so that it's doubled.
- Make your children aware of their position in a global context. The chances are pretty good that if you can read this book, your children have way more resources than at least 70 percent of the children in the world.

- Find out what your children care about, and volunteer your time in this area as well as the areas you are interested in.

A U.S. organization called Learning to Give is developing curriculum materials to teach children how to give in order to encourage giving in society. The organization's goal is to deliver these resources to children and teachers. You can download the materials for free from their Web site (see the resource list at the back of the book).

GIVING YOUR CHILDREN HEART FIBER

Parents and other adults have a great opportunity to give a special gift to children, something that we call heart fiber. When you give a child heart fiber, you are giving him or her the values and virtues that build a strong character.

Just as your body needs fiber to maintain its strength, your heart needs fiber to maintain its strength in a world where you are buffeted each day by problems and injustices. When you help children build strong hearts, full of empathy, they are better able to survive the many challenges they will undoubtedly encounter. When children confront a difficult choice, one that might involve harm to themselves or others, heart fiber will get them through safely.

The CORE parts of heart fiber are

Compassion
Order (Self-control)
Respect
Empathy

When children develop these qualities, they become giving citizens who are both happier and healthier than those who lack heart fiber. Strong heart fiber will unleash their generosity, kindness, and community involvement.

How do children develop heart fiber? They learn it from their environment, their peers, and their community, but the most important factor is their parents. It doesn't matter if children grow up in poverty or in difficult circumstances. As long as they have at least one adult in their lives who loves them unconditionally, who supports them and helps them build on their strengths, these children will grow up with heart fiber.

As any parent knows, raising a child is one of the most difficult jobs you will ever have. The hours are long, there's no financial reimbursement, and the pain can be significant. On the other hand, no reward is greater than seeing the child whom you love and who loves you go out into the world full of courage and compassion.

Michele Borba in *Building Moral Intelligence: The Seven Essential Virtues That Teach Kids to Do the Right Thing* says that "moral intelligence is learned and you can start building it when your children are toddlers." In her book, she offers many practical ideas that parents can implement to help protect their children from the toxic forces in our culture. In addition, she helps parents realize the important role they play in shaping their children and developing their heart fiber.

community

Our various communities, based on geography (where we live), faith (our religious institutions), culture, politics, family, workplace, etc., are where we live our lives. They are places where we learn, love, express ourselves, and feel connected to something bigger than ourselves.

Communities become stronger when members make a commitment to become involved and connect with others. They are also a place where we can perfect our skills and practice giving. Azim honed his leadership and speaking skills by volunteering time in his community. He has gained as much as he has given, although that was not his intention.

Then there is Harvey's friend Rebecca Hughes. Rebecca made a spontaneous decision when she was two months pregnant. She was standing in the elevator of the large apartment building where she lived when she noticed a woman about eight months pregnant. Rebecca blurted out: "I see you're pregnant. I am too! What if we exchange babysitting?" She scrawled her number on a scrap of paper and placed it in the hand of the other woman, who looked shocked. However, a week later the woman called Rebecca and said, "I've been thinking about it. How would you like to start exchanging now? You could start racking up hours of my help even before your baby is born." Rebecca quickly accepted her offer.

Soon she and her new friend invited several other moms to join their group. Each woman was giving to a number of others what they most needed at the time: support, knowledge, love, care, and the very precious naps that many of them desperately needed during the day.

Because of their weekly playgroup, the mothers were able to enjoy adult company, and a good group of children they knew and trusted became their children's community. Eventually, twenty families were involved in this group. The co-op quickly became indispensable for many of the women involved.

The beauty of Rebecca's random act of giving is that she took a risk. The risk she took was to get involved with someone she didn't know and to hope that they could build a mutually beneficial relationship. Rebecca's wisdom was to take the risk instead of accepting being isolated, as so many people do in society today. As it turned out, the risk was small, but the benefits were great.

Paul Loeb tells Rebecca's story in *Soul of a Citizen*. Stories like Rebecca's occur every day in every part of the world. When a person realizes that a group response is more powerful than isolated individuals acting alone, a community starts to grow.

Harvey's neighbors, Susan and Patrick Faehndrich, decided they wanted to get to know other people in their community. In rainy places like Vancouver, people spend a lot of time indoors, so it is often hard to connect with neighbors. In addition, they live in a multicultural community where the majority of individuals have limited fluency in English.

Susan decided that a good way to engage people would be to build community gardens at the end of each block. She convinced enough neighbors to spend a number of evenings and Saturdays building the gardens, cleaning up the garbage in the area, and securing donated seeds and tools. Eventually, there were gardens and benches at the end of three blocks in her neighborhood.

It proved to be a fabulous way for people to meet one another, to build trust in the neighborhood, to understand what was going on in different ethnic communities, and to help protect everybody in the neighborhood. When people know their neighbors, communities are much safer. The benefits arising from

Susan's and Patrick's gifts of energy, time, and skills have been tremendous.

Building a community requires that you take risks and invest time and energy. Not every individual you try to engage will be receptive. There may be many good reasons why they aren't, but the key factor in creating communities is the willingness to take a risk. With the help of others, you can leverage your own giving many times over.

Loeb writes: "Our most serious problems, both the public ones and those that seem most personal, are in large part common problems, which can be solved only through common efforts. The dream of private sanctuary is an illusion. It erodes our souls by eroding our sense of larger connection, whether to our fellow human beings or to that force many of us call God. The walls we're building around ourselves, around those closest to us, and ultimately around our hearts, may provide a temporary feeling of security. But they can't prevent the world from affecting us. Quite the opposite."

Even though they want to give, some people occasionally have feelings of despair, hopelessness, or inadequacy. They want to have a positive impact on the world but feel they have had little success. We can assure you that every time you take an action to make the world a better place, there is some small benefit, even if you can't measure it at the time.

If everyone gives in to feelings of hopelessness and becomes immobilized, there is no doubt that people of ill will and greed will control society. Though we strongly believe that this group is a small minority, we also believe the individual actions of good men and women are critical to society's health.

Loeb's research on communities reveals that the main distinction between those who participate fully in their community (and therefore give more) and those who withdraw into private life is that active citizens learn a key lesson: You don't have to wait for the perfect circumstances, perfect cause, or perfect level of knowledge to take a stand. Proceed step by step. Don't get overwhelmed before you start, and try to enjoy the process of engagement as much as the objective itself.

Author Elbert Hubbard once said, "There is no failure except in no longer trying." Don't give up if you want to make a difference in other people's lives.

GIVING TO ELDERS

In a crowded, busy world, many people have severed the connection with their elders. We believe these people are poorer for this broken connection, as are their elders. Both of us grew up with many older family members in our lives, and we considered it a blessing.

When children have the opportunity to spend time with their grandparents, they often do not realize what a great gift it is. Only when they reach middle age does it become apparent how valuable and meaningful this time can be. The older people in their lives brought them into the world, cared for them, taught them, and loved them, but only when they become parents do they realize how much their elders loved them.

After Azim had children of his own, his parents and grandmother came to live with the family. Azim's daughter, Sahar, was three at the time. And sixteen years later, she still remembers how her grandmother cared for Sahar's great-grandmother, who was very ill. It was a chance to watch "giving in action."

Both Sahar and her brother, Tawfiq, have lived with their grandparents (Azim's mom and dad) for most of their life. Azim's wife, Farzana, has lost both of her parents, but she was able to give of her caring to her in-laws and receive their love in return. The children get a chance to receive wisdom and unconditional love from their grandparents, and the grandparents maintain a sense of youthfulness and receive joy from being around their grandchildren. Azim is thankful to witness this blessing and to express gratitude for having supportive family members who believe in the power of giving. Times are not always perfect, but overall it has been beneficial to the entire family.

People must not underestimate the enthusiasm and vigor of the young or the experience and wisdom of the elderly, which can provide them with great life lessons. Keeping family values strong across the generations has many benefits for all parties involved, and it's never too late to reconnect disconnected family ties.

You might want to consider offering the gift of your time to seniors who are not part of your biological family. Many seniors are lonely. Their children and grandchildren are scattered, often living far away. Acts of kindness such as stopping to say hello, taking time to talk with them, helping them with groceries, or sharing a coffee are meaningful gifts. These gifts can also help you to slow down, to reflect on life, and to learn something new. Elders deserve your attention and respect because they're part of your "family," defined more broadly. Try to incorporate this form of giving into your life.

THE BROADER COMMUNITY

Harvey had been thinking about social involvement for a while before he took action. When he realized that he would never do anything if he waited for the "perfect" time, Harvey got involved in anti-apartheid work. He was in his late teens when he helped organize boycotts of South African products. This was back in 1971, when only a few people seemed to be interested in the issue.

As he grew older and gained more skills (partly owing to this volunteer work), Harvey moved to large organizations where he arranged film tours about South Africa, set up university boycotts, and even made the national television news with an anti-apartheid campaign he and a friend had launched. Harvey devoted thousands of hours, helped raise many millions of dollars for anti-apartheid activity, and helped produce the award-winning film *In Darkest Hollywood: Cinema and Apartheid.*

Over the years, a rapidly growing number of people were carrying out similar actions all over the world. This work, led by South Africans of all races, helped to topple the apartheid regime in 1989.

As a result of the time and energy he put into the anti-apartheid campaign, Harvey managed to make great lifelong friends, become sensitive to racism in himself and his own society, and learn a lot about the world. He also developed many skills. And he is certain that he received more in return than he gave.

Big tasks—such as stopping torture around the world, eliminating land mines, or fighting against gambling addiction—are tremendously difficult and require that millions of people around the world make a commitment to help solve the problems that affect so many. But positive changes happen. Many of the social problems that existed decades ago have been, if not solved, at least partially resolved, and there is much more justice in our world because of communal effort.

If you don't think that one person, or a single act or gesture, can make a difference, you need only remember Rosa Parks, the black woman in the racially segregated southern United States, who refused to give up her seat on the bus to a white person. Her simple but courageous act started a chain of events that changed the future for millions of black Americans. Similarly, decades ago women had very few opportunities compared to those they have today. Now, thanks to the women and men who fought to gain a place for women in what used to be male-only occupations, most jobs are now open to both sexes, and frequently more than half the students in formerly male-dominated graduate, medical, and law schools are women.

History is full of small groups of people who have initiated creative and positive changes in our world. As Margaret Mead said, "Never doubt that a small group of thoughtful, committed citizens can change the world. Indeed, it's the only thing that ever has."

GIVING GLOBALLY

You've probably never been awakened at midnight by gunfire and screaming. Five-year-old Jorge has. He had no idea what was happening when he woke up. His mother shouted for him to run. Holding hands with his older sister, he ran out of his home into the African night. He never saw his mother and father again.

Jorge is a war orphan. His village in Mozambique was attacked by a group of guerrillas during his country's civil war. They burned his home and kidnapped, tortured, or murdered everyone they found in his village. Luckily, Jorge and his sister managed to escape. Traveling with their uncle, they walked for nine dreadful days to reach safety. They survived those nine days because of the incredible generosity of other Mozambicans, who are among the poorest people in the world. These people shared what little food, clothing, and water they had, to ensure that the refugees reached a place where they could rebuild their lives.

A few years ago Harvey met Jorge in his new village, where Jorge lived with six hundred other refugees, mostly children, many of them orphans. One of every two children was dying from either disease or malnutrition. The refugees, adults and children, escaped with nothing. No food, no possessions. But Oxfam, the development agency that Harvey worked for at the time, provided emergency clothing and, more important, the tools and seeds needed to begin subsistence farming so the villagers could rebuild their lives. Harvey met them about six months after they arrived in their new home.

You can imagine the people's pride as they showed off the maize and beans they were growing. They were feeding themselves! Jorge's uncle explained that the children were still hungry, but their health had already started to improve.

And what did it cost? Not much. Just fifteen dollars—the price of a CD—bought enough seeds and tools to make it possible for a family to grow its own food. There are many international development agencies like Oxfam doing this kind of practical, self-help work every day: UNICEF, United Nations High Commission for Refugees (UNHCR), Alternatives, Action Aid, Mercy Corps, Médecins sans Frontières (MSF), and The Aga Khan Foundation. A long list of groups helps the one-quarter of humanity that exists on a dollar a day. And every day these groups help people to improve their own lives.

During Azim's trip to Pakistan and Afghanistan, he visited

many Afghan families. Each time he arrived at another home, the family would offer their best food to him and the other volunteers. Azim and his colleagues knew that these people hardly had enough to eat themselves, let alone extra to feed guests. However, it was their custom to feed their *mehman*—a guest in their house—and they always kept some food for that purpose. To Azim, this was an amazing act of giving.

People at all levels of income, wealth, and status can give according to their abilities, whether they give small amounts of food, money, time, or energy.

When you give to people living on the edge of survival, you know that the help you give creates hope. We believe that if there is any hope for the world to grow less unkind and even less brutal, this hope comes from the actions of people like you. Charity may begin at home, but the world is your home and all citizens are your neighbors. We urge you, therefore, to consider giving to people in the poorest parts of the world. Imagine what just one of your dollars is worth when exchanged for currency in the developing world—it is the daily salary for more than one billion people.

GIVING TO NONPROFIT SOCIAL ORGANIZATIONS

Nonprofit organizations are the channel through which most people give money and time to important causes. Each of the millions of nonprofits in the world was created because of a need, and every year thousands of new nonprofits are formed.

Here's the story of how one new organization was born. In Latin America and the Caribbean there is frequently a lack of medical expertise, technology, and money to access health care. But parents of children whose lives are at risk do what they can to help their child. Many of them moved to Florida, and they began showing up at Holtz Children's Hospital, part of the Jackson Memorial Medical Center at the University of Miami.

Rolando Rodriguez, director of the Jackson Memorial Hospital Foundation, was disturbed by the number of families that were coming to the hospital, begging him to help their children. How could he say no? In response, the foundation set up the International Kids Fund to help these kids from Latin America and the Caribbean get the treatment they need.

A child suffering with cancer is one of the saddest things in the world. Robert Arias, a five-year-old from the Dominican Republic, had leukemia. His doctor, Rosa Nieves, told Robert's parents there was nothing else she could do for him, but she offered them a ray of hope when she told them about the International Kids Fund.

The good news: Little Robert Arias received treatment, and today he's back home in the Dominican Republic, as healthy as any other seven-year-old. We're sure you can imagine how grateful his parents are. They found hope when it seemed as if there was none.

We can't list all the world's nonprofit groups, but we've included a few generic types of nonprofits in the box Types of Nonprofit Groups.

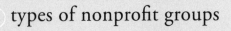

types of nonprofit groups

You can choose from an incredible variety of nonprofit organizations, including:

International development agencies
Environmental groups
Mental health services
Refugee and immigrant assistance agencies
Women's shelters
Faith groups
Hospitals
Colleges
Arts organizations
Hospices
Food banks
Research organizations
Peace groups
Legal-aid groups
Animal protection groups
Groups working for global justice
Alternative media
Antiracism organizations
Antipoverty organizations
Aid to low-income families
Missions
Service organizations for minorities

And of course you can find more information about any type of charity in your community, by searching online, in the Yellow Pages or your mail, or by asking your friends. It has never been easier to discover a cause that appeals to your heart.

With so many needy (and worthy) causes, how do you decide where to give your money? In chapter four we'll give you some tips to help sort out the many options so that you can give where you and the cause benefit most. But the core reason to give is always an emotional one: The cause simply touched your heart.

SMALL ORGANIZATIONS CAN HAVE A BIG IMPACT

There are many good causes you can give to. Many people think first of the large well-known organizations, but we ask you to consider small local organizations also—day cares, hospices, women's shelters—and we ask you to consider giving time as well as money. This is because small groups often make a huge difference.

For example, every time you get on an airplane and aren't breathing secondhand smoke, you have a small Canadian non-profit to thank. Flying in an airplane fifteen years ago was a smoky, unpleasant experience for many passengers. Usually about a quarter of the passengers would be smoking, and because of poor ventilation systems, passengers had to breathe significant amounts of secondhand smoke in a small enclosed space. When you got off the plane your clothes reeked of smoke, and often you would have a headache. It was an uncomfortable way to travel. But Garfield Mahood and the Non-Smokers' Rights Association based in Toronto promoted an aggressive clean-indoor-air revolution. This ultimately led to Air Canada becoming the first airline in the world to ban in-flight smoking. This started a chain reaction that forced all major carriers to ban smoking. Today, even many smokers appreciate the smoke-free air on an airplane.

The Non-Smokers' Rights Association has just two thousand donors, yet it has been called the best tobacco-control group in the world, and for good reason. It has championed many initiatives, like Canada's world precedent–setting tobacco package warnings, which have dramatically reduced the number of smokers in Canada and have influenced policy and laws in many other countries. The association's work will help extend the lives of hundreds of thousands of individuals around the world.

Another small organization that has made a big impact in many countries is the Planned Lifetime Advocacy Network (PLAN). Started by Al Etmanski, a leading advocate for people with developmental disabilities, PLAN's strategy is to help develop a circle of friends for a person with special needs. This circle could include neighbors, relatives, and other individuals who care about the person with the disability. The support network is designed to last for decades. This long-term support is especially important for aging parents of a child with a mental handicap. What the parents want most in the world, after all, is to know their child will be taken care of when they are gone.

Yet another reason to consider giving to small organizations is that you can be more connected with their mission, their actions, and their accomplishments. You can see firsthand how they help people or the environment. You can see where they do well and where they need to improve, and channeling your skills or money may be all that is needed to help them do better. In short, sometimes you can have a greater impact with your time or money in a small group than in a larger organization.

Of course, there are also many reasons to give to larger organizations because with their size and scope they have the capacity to make significant changes in certain situations. But don't forget the small groups.

giving to our planet

Every major world faith teaches the concept of stewardship, which could be called care of creation. Humans have been entrusted with great resources: water, air, land, animals, and food from many plants. Every faith teaches what many people already know intuitively: Humans must protect these resources. And yet, how many fish stocks have people depleted? How many animals have disappeared forever? How many habitats have humans destroyed by clear-cutting or by poisoning the land and water?

A few years ago Harvey made a film about the environmental crisis in the Black Sea. He learned that of the twenty-six species of fish in the Black Sea, twenty-three had been fished to extinction. In the north Atlantic, nearly all the cod—the greatest fishing resource in history—have disappeared due to overfishing.

Oceans are being emptied. Rivers are being polluted. Air makes people sick. Food is full of antibiotics and pesticides. At the core of these problems you'll find greed and selfishness, which means a person's self-interest is more important than the interest of the majority.

For thousands of years, humans converted the resources of the earth into energy, harvested forests, grew crops, fished oceans, etc., in a way that was sustainable. This is no longer the case. Now humans are depleting natural capital (the water, the air, the earth) faster than it can regenerate itself. People are changing the climate through excessive use of fossil fuels. Humans do many positive things to protect the earth but do incredibly destructive things as well.

As the prominent scientist David Suzuki laments, "We've contaminated the air, water and soil, driven wild things to extinction, torn down the ancient forests, poisoned the rain and ripped holes in the heavens. Prosperity of the industrial world has been purchased at the expense of our children's future."

It's time to see protection of the environment as an issue for all people. It's not a right-wing or a left-wing issue—it's a human issue. When people damage the environment, others must challenge their actions and make certain that they are held accountable for what they do. If people alive today work together to protect the environment, it will give future generations a chance to survive with clean water and air.

We believe it is time to start giving back and taking care of the planet. As we noted, every faith tradition teaches care of creation. But most people are not aware of these traditions or fail to practice them in their daily lives. Actions arising from this ignorance have a major negative impact on the planet and its resources.

Because we both have young children, we often ask ourselves what kind of world we are leaving for them. What kind of air, water, and land are we bequeathing to our grandchildren? We can be gracious, generous, and kind in our giving, but if the only home we have is being damaged at a rapid rate, we all have to take quick action. The really devastating consequences of human damage to the environment, which will become more evident in the decades to come, won't have as much impact on us as it will have on our children. That's why we want you to hear about what is happening to our environment from a child—a child who may well be wiser than most adults.

At the age of thirteen, Severn Suzuki (daughter of David Suzuki) wrote a speech that she delivered to world leaders at the 1993 Global Forum in Kyoto, Japan. Severn brought the room to tears with her honest, powerful, and prescient words.

"I've sat through six days of sessions of the Global Forum," she began, "and have noticed two things about all the discussions I've listened to: they are *very* complicated and, I hope you'll excuse me for saying this, but to me, the decisions made didn't seem important enough. . . . I guess my life and ideas are pretty simple and straightforward, but watching you struggle to find how to change values, I wonder sometimes if adults, in their complicated work and lives, forget the *simple* things. . . .

"I am willing to share and to give things up—I have plenty. But people and governments that have more than enough seem unwilling to share with the needy. Everybody says they are all for peace and happiness, but there are billions of dollars that could go to ending poverty and reducing pollution and environmental problems that are being spent on weapons to kill and destroy.

"I've tried to help save rain forests and rivers and animals, but the argument I get is that people have to have a healthy economy *first*.

"But you can't eat money! And you can't make a living if there are no fish, no forests, no Nature to live on. Money can never replace our *real* necessities . . .

"You grownups tell us how we should behave. You tell us not to fight, to clean up our mess, not to hurt other creatures, to share, not be greedy. Then you go and do the things you tell us not to do. . . .

"Because you are our models, we try to be like you, so please be the way you should be. Sometimes I think grownups have forgotten that it's OK to be brave! It's OK to be different. You keep telling children not to pay attention to what other kids say about us, not to be a follower. Why are *you* afraid to lead? What will your legacy be to us? And when I copy you, what will I leave for the generations to come?"

If a thirteen-year-old can try to tackle the hardest issues of the twenty-first century, so can you. You have skills, experience, and resources that can be used. You just need to decide to use them in meaningful ways. By taking action to protect the environment, you are giving the great gift of life to future generations of all living things—plants, animals, and humans.

Who should you give to first? Yourself? Your family? Your community? To nonprofit organizations? To your planet? How do you set your priorities? Do you feel it's an either/or situation because of lack of time? We hope that by reading this chapter you will come upon an abundant mentality—that the more you give, the more you create.

key points

Charity begins at home. Start by loving yourself. It is not wrong to give to yourself. To look after others, you have to look after yourself first.

Make a conscious effort to give daily to your family. It forms the foundation of your giving.

Children hold the power to make our world better and our future bright and peaceful. The best gift we can give our children is to teach them to give.

We build heart fiber in our children by giving them the values and virtues that build a strong character.

Extend your giving to your community.

Give to nonprofit social organizations. There is an incredible variety of options for giving.

Give to the planet—it has been given to us in trust. We must take care of our environment to be able to pass on to our children what our ancestors gave us.

how, when, where, and how much to give

Now we get down to the practicalities of how to give, when to give, where to give (which cause or organization), and how much to give.

First, we emphasize the importance of giving with respect, giving with humility, and giving unconditionally. Then, we describe when to give. Surprisingly, you can give even in times of hardship.

Many people have trouble deciding where is the best place to give their time, money, skills, or other resources. We've included several exercises you can do to determine where your heart leads you.

Finally, we discuss how much to give, including a consideration of tithing. We also suggest that you will have more to give if you strive for balance and simplicity in your life. It is important to balance giving with receiving, giving to others with giving to your family and to yourself, and giving locally with giving to solve "big picture" problems.

how to give

If your hand always remains in your pocket, you can never shake hands with others. You can't offer a hand of compassion. You can't give a tender touch of love. You can't grow as a human until you first learn to remove your hands from your pockets. When your hand offers a gift of money to help a child, to protect the environment, or to bring more justice to the world, you personally share the benefits of giving.

Giving in any way is usually better than not giving at all. However, when you give with your heart, it is very powerful. The receiver gets to feel that sincerity, depth, connection, and impact. Poet and philosopher Kahlil Gibran says, "To live in the hearts of others is not to die." This happens when you give with the heart. Let your heart be your beacon in the dark.

We give when we act in a positive and healthy manner. Each time we are upbeat, kind, and loving, we share positive energy. Each time we are negative, we send out negative energies. It takes less effort to be positive than to be negative.

Giving possessions is good. However, giving of yourself has more impact. When you give your possessions, the gifts may be temporary and short-lived. When you give of yourself to others, the benefits they reap are sustained. You reward those who gave of themselves to you for a long time, even after they have died.

We all have an enormous capacity to give. By dreaming big for our giving, not only are we able to give more but we also create a similar outlook in other facets of our life, including our work. Motivational author Robert Schuller asks, "What would you attempt to do if you knew you could not fail?" Our beliefs and imagination create our reality. The gift of thinking big in giving can be passed to our children and the younger generation, creating a better world for all.

GIVE WITH RESPECT

All human beings need to be respected. One of the ways of giving is to show respect to all people, regardless of their social status, gender, age, or religion. As Kahlil Gibran says, "The wind does not blow more sweetly to the giant oak than it does to the least blade of grass."

One way to show deep respect is to listen attentively. When you listen actively, you understand the person talking to you much better and so are able to communicate better. This lets the other person feel validated, understood, and perhaps even loved.

When Azim was serving as a volunteer on the social welfare board, he learned very quickly that it was not what he said that made a difference. It was how attentively he listened. Once, after a two-hour conversation, a client was dissatisfied because Azim spoke more than he listened. In another instance, Azim listened attentively for twenty minutes without saying much, and the client was totally satisfied. Listening is a form of great respect to others, and everyone can give this gift at no cost.

Another way to give with respect is to give in a manner that empowers the recipient. By empowering other people, you make them self-sufficient, which helps to preserve their dignity.

With so much strife and commotion in the world, people feel vulnerable and scared. Nations do not trust one another. People of one religion look down upon people of other religions. It would be a great gift if every person, in his or her own way, showed respect for people of different countries, cultures, and faiths. Believing that diversity is a strength, not a weakness, gives people an opportunity to expand their perspectives. They learn from each other and care for each other.

Indeed, one of the ways to bring harmony to the world is through enhanced pluralism. Pluralism means that you realize there are many paths to the truth. There is not just one right way. The tree has many branches and leaves, but the roots are the same: We come from the same source and we inhabit the same planet. We face the same challenges of being human. Pluralism means actively promoting tolerance, understanding, and respect.

While you may worship a God different from that of your neighbors or worship no God at all, there are lessons you can learn from every faith tradition. Every faith promotes giving of your heart, time, and wealth. What you give does not have to be an object or to have any tangible value. Our heartfelt giving is frequently in words—not words from our mouth but words from our heart.

GIVE WITH HUMILITY

One of the best ways to give is with utmost humility. Not everyone knows how to give or even gets a chance to give. So when you get an opportunity to give, do not hesitate. Take it with both hands and give of yourself with respect, dignity, and compassion.

Compassion has been defined as "your pain in my heart." You can feel someone's pain in your heart when you have taken the time to listen carefully and attentively. Compassion starts with ourselves—we need to listen to ourselves to be aware of our deep thoughts.

Compassion and humility come about when we practice another great giving habit: being nonjudgmental. Rumi says, "Beyond right doing and wrong doing there is a field. Meet me there." If you are humble and respectful, you will refrain from judging other people. You will realize that the way you see the world is not how the world is but how you are; how you see others is more a reflection of you than of them!

Everyone you meet is trying their best in the only way they know how. Plato said, "Be kind, for everyone is fighting a hard battle." A goal for each of us could be to give people the benefit of the doubt and be nonjudgmental. Instead, be there for people when they need you. When you lend your hand to others, the universe lends its hand to you. You invite abundance into your life.

The universe and nature, after all, do not judge—they just provide lessons and consequences.

GIVE UNCONDITIONALLY

If you give because you want credit for what you have done, it reduces the impact of giving. Remember, true giving is unconditional! Nature gives unconditionally. The flower gives its fragrance, and the sun its light, without seeking anything in return. True love is to love others not because they are lovable or because they love you but simply because you love. The very act of unconditional giving is the reward because it is also a gift to yourself.

In the words of Ralph Waldo Emerson, "It is one of the beautiful compensations of this life that no one can sincerely try to help another without helping himself."

when to give

The short answer is . . . today.

Some people believe that they can give only when things are going well. The reality is that you can give at all times. If you give when you are hurt or when you are in hardship, you sometimes create the energy that can help you through your hard time. That is the power of giving for the giver!

Sometimes you might say, "I'll give when I've got lots to give." Unfortunately, it doesn't often work that way. Imagine you decide to give 10 percent of your income and are finding it hard to part with $100 from $1,000. How will you feel when you have to part with $10,000 from $100,000? Or $100,000 from $1,000,000? If you do not establish the habit of giving, it will be very hard to give, even when you have more.

You may think you don't have a lot to give away. You may even say, "Well, if I had as much as Bill Gates, of course I'd give a lot away." But comparing yourself to others is often an unhealthy act. Either you feel bad or you feel superior. Neither is a positive emotion.

Look at your own situation. Are there areas where you can

spend less money without dramatically affecting your life? If you have very little money, you can give time instead.

In some cases, even giving time can be difficult. Your family might be upset with you for being away from the house too much and for not carrying your load. Here you must strive for balance, or you may end up giving in a way that hurts more than it helps. You also have to assess whether you are in the right place offering the right contribution.

Having said this, we believe that no matter what or how much you give, when you give wholeheartedly and with good intentions, you set in motion a powerful force. And if nothing else, you'll experience instantaneous satisfaction. In that regard, giving is priceless! Why not take a minute now to make a list of what you can give and when?

GIVING IN HARDSHIP
Giving in hardship makes it easier to give when times are good. Giving in hardship can also sometimes ease the hardship and produce unexpected results.

While waiting for a friend at the airport, Azim met a woman who was also waiting. She shared with him a powerful story about her young brother and her encounter with death.

This woman's brother was born into her family after the parents had spent many years wishing for a son. Shortly after the birth of her brother, this woman had to leave for England to study. She did not have much contact with her brother, except during the short visits she made to Vancouver. This continued until her brother became very sick and was critically ill. The sister then flew home from England and spent six weeks with her brother in the hospital before he died. The woman told Azim that in the six weeks she remained by her brother's bed, she bonded with him so deeply that she described it as the best six weeks in her life. She said that even though she misses her brother, the memories of those six weeks are so powerful that she is going to be forever grateful for that experience.

When Azim shared this story with a group of people fighting cancer, one woman related a similar story about how she had spent three weeks with her mother before her mom died. She said it was the most intimate time she had ever had with her mother.

Now how is it that these three or six weeks can be more powerful than a relationship that may have lasted sixty years? We believe these magical experiences happen because there is a powerful giving and receiving happening at a very deep level during these hardships. Closed hearts can be opened by deep pain.

In times of hardship, you sometimes focus on your problems and become totally self-centered. But when you become more giving, you escape from feelings of self-centeredness and create a new kind of positive, rewarding energy. When you give, you feel abundant. This feeling creates a self-fulfilling prophecy.

Kahlil Gibran says, "Someone who has hurt you is also hurting; maybe with your kindness this hurt will go away." Sometimes you are hurt, and the last thing you want to do is give, especially to someone who has hurt you. But maybe that person is hurting too. People often hurt others because they themselves are hurting. Their pain does not justify their actions, of course, but it does help you understand why they do what they do.

Sometimes when you do not feel like giving at all, you may need to start by giving to yourself. Start by forcing yourself to smile at a stranger or even at yourself! It will help you to relax and make you feel better. The day you are able to feel joy in giving, no matter what your status, is the day you will find bliss in life. As this Sufi saying reminds us: "When our joy in affliction equals our joy in blessing, we have found the true meaning of life."

where to give

There are three areas that you need to evaluate before you can decide where you want to direct your time, money, and other gifts. These areas are

- your emotions, values, and motivations
- your skills, and
- the other resources you have to give (time, connections, and so on).

In this section, we provide practical steps to help you evaluate these areas. Then, we describe what most nonprofits need before suggesting ways to match your assets with them.

EMOTIONS, VALUES, AND MOTIVATIONS

To evaluate your emotions, values, and motivation, ask yourself the following questions:

- What moves me emotionally?
- What makes me sad, happy, angry, inspired, fearful, loving, and passionate?

Really think about your answers. They will help you choose the causes you feel most strongly about and to which you should give the most. As philanthropist and entrepreneur Paul Brainerd says, "Discover where your own heartfelt passions lie; focus your energy in those areas. I think that's really important. There are so many things out there that are needy causes but you have to feel that heartfelt passion and then decide how you want to apply it. And everyone can make a difference and the question for you is, *How do you want to give back?*"

How do you determine what you care about most? Focus is difficult when we are buffeted by competing desires to help. The exercise "Why Do I Want to Give?" will help you focus.

why do i want to give?

Close your eyes and breathe for two minutes. Relax your mind and body. After a couple of minutes of relaxation, think about what moves you emotionally. What makes you angry, sad, happy, passionate? Where do you think you could help the most?

Hold these emotions and then dictate or write out what went through your mind and heart. List what problems you would like to see eliminated. List those issues you feel need to be addressed.

You should also think about what is important to you when you give. We've listed a few ideas below, but there could be hundreds of options on this list. List what is important to you.

- I want to feel better.
- I like to make a difference.
- I want to protect our environment.
- I like to help kids.
- I believe good education is a fundamental right.
- I believe we have to care for animals.

(Go to our Web site at www.thepowerofgiving.org/whats_important.html and add your personal favorite to this list.)

After this assessment, you can set priorities. What are the top three areas that you care about? Or, for that matter, what is your top priority? Which one is the easiest for you to engage in? For instance, your highest priority may be to work directly with poor people in Africa, but this may not be realistic given your circumstances. If your second-highest priority is working with poor people in your own community, this could become the focus of your volunteering effort.

SKILLS

The next step is to evaluate your skills. You can do this on your own, with a friend, or with a group. The benefit of having a friend or two do this with you is that he or she will often be a more positive judge of what you have to offer.

The list "What Nonprofits Need Most" catalogs some of the resources and skills that many organizations need. It might help you identify skills you have that you didn't think of as valuable.

what nonprofits need most

- People with the following special skills:
  - accounting
  - fund-raising
  - management
  - personnel
  - publicity
  - marketing
  - writing
  - public speaking
  - other languages
  - leadership
  - organizing
  - design (for print, posters, and Web sites)
- Volunteers for the board of directors
- Office administration assistants
- Volunteers for special events and fund-raising
- Volunteers who can give educational presentations to groups about issues/the group's mission
- Volunteer counselors (e.g., for AIDS groups, women's shelters, crisis centers)

- Volunteers with tech skills to keep computers running
- People with experience and connections

Many organizations also need the following resources:

- Money, particularly donations that are not earmarked for a specific purpose (i.e., general funds to cover whatever is needed)
- Phones
- Computer equipment
- Old printing equipment
- Old copying equipment
- Staff time
- Meeting space
- Vehicles
- Other specialty services such as food, billboards, banners, etc.
- Sponsorship
- Matching grants

Obviously, many other skills would be useful. Whether it is giving massages or growing food, any of your skills or experience might be useful for giving. Try to come up with as many as possible, and then think about special abilities you have in each skill category. For example, if you have experience in organizing, what are you particularly good at organizing?

- offices
- events
- parties
- other volunteers

WHAT OTHER RESOURCES CAN YOU OFFER?

Now that you have an idea of the skills you have and the area in which you want to apply them, you have to decide how much you can realistically give.

Do you have spare time? How much spare time do you think you have each week? Is there a time of year when you have a block of time to offer?

What else can you offer? (See the list titled "What Nonprofits Need Most" for some ideas.)

Can the company you work for donate money, people, or other resources?

Are you connected to people of influence in your various communities? Can you draw on their skills to help out a cause you believe in, or can you have them help you develop your own skills?

PUTTING IT ALL TOGETHER

Now that you have evaluated your emotions, values, and motivations, and have identified the skills, time, and other resources that you might be able to give, we suggest you decide on your giving priorities.

You can pick one particular issue and devote most of your giving (in the form of time, wisdom, money, skills, connections, and so on) to it. If you become a significant donor, this might earn you an invitation to sit on the board and have more influence.

Alternatively, you can select a variety of causes, which means you will support a number of areas. For instance, you could volunteer at your child's school, sit on the board of an organization that helps people with special needs, donate to an environmental group, and walk or cycle rather than drive your car to work (this last example gives in two ways: you give yourself better health and you "give" to the environment by protecting the air around you).

Of the resources you can offer, which would be most useful to the individuals or groups you want to give to? List them in order of their value to others.

(The skills or resources needed vary from group to group and depend on their mission, size, and current resources. Talk to a board member or staff member to find out how you can contribute most effectively.)

How you give depends on your personality and priorities. Your priorities can, and likely will, change over time, so it's worth reevaluating these once a year. You may also need to get more information on the causes you're interested in to decide where you'll ultimately direct your skills and resources. "Evaluating Nonprofits" raises a few issues you should consider when selecting a nonprofit you'd like to help.

evaluating nonprofits

You should try to find the answers to the following questions when you are considering giving to a specific nonprofit:

- Is the nonprofit effective?
- What percentage of your donation goes to administration?
- Can you see where your gift helps?
- Does the nonprofit have good leadership?
- Is the group tackling the symptoms or the root causes of a problem?

It's obviously important that a nonprofit's vision and values match yours.

There are a number of ways to evaluate nonprofits. Most have Web sites, and you should be able to find information there. Alternatively, you can talk to a board member, a staff member, or a volunteer. You can also ask friends what they think about particular causes, especially local ones.

Most nonprofits produce annual reports, including audited financial statements, which are posted on their Web sites. Organizations that share these with the public have already demonstrated a positive degree of transparency.

There are Web sites that evaluate larger charities in the United States. The URLs for these sites are included in the resource list at the end of the book.

When you examine a nonprofit's annual report or other

promotional material (Web sites, brochures, etc.), you should consider its track record and its measurement of activities compared to goals. The composition of a board of directors often gives you a sense of the nonprofit's direction, leadership, and even integrity. For instance, if an environmental organization has a prominent scientist on its board, this likely indicates that its work will be more science-based.

When you give to a nonprofit, you are investing your time or money. It's good to be strategic and focused so you can have the maximum impact, even if you can give only a small amount of time, money, or other resources. Spending a little time doing research will give you confidence that you've made a good decision.

Remember that your decision doesn't have to be perfect. You'll learn how to improve your giving by giving.

One last note: Just because a nonprofit spends more on administration or fund-raising expenses than another nonprofit does not necessarily make it less attractive. Newer organizations often have to spend more on administration or fund-raising while they work to build a base of committed donors. This shouldn't deter you from supporting them if they fill an important need.

Moreover, an organization with low administration expenses may not carefully monitor how donations are spent. For example, a group could spend 20 percent on administration to ensure that a project effectively achieves its goals. And another group could spend just 10 percent on administration.

(continued)

However, the second group may need to spend more money overall to achieve the same outcome if expenditures are not effectively distributed or monitored. There is always a balance, and some groups may simply invest money more wisely, even if it appears as an administration cost.

There are some nonprofits that have voluntary help that look after the administration. This would reduce costs. Again, it's a good idea to investigate to be certain that the volunteers are capable of overseeing the administration of the money.

Due diligence will help you find out which nonprofit is effectively using your donation for your desired objective.

how much to give

Obviously, how much you can give is related to your personal circumstances. A single mother of three children may not have much time or money to give, but by helping take care of a friend's child during an emergency, she makes a generous contribution to a person in need.

A core question to ask yourself is "Where can I have the maximum impact with my giving?" The answer to this question is key to enhancing your personal satisfaction from giving and to maximizing the benefits to the recipients of your generosity.

Let's examine two of the gifts that most people offer: money and time.

Craig O'Brian believes in tithing—giving one-tenth of his

income. In fact, one of his goals is to give much more than 10 percent of his income. He's a minister at a Baptist church in Vancouver, Canada, and he believes many faith groups spend too much on their own institutions and not enough serving those with the greatest needs. He devotes much of his time to causes that are not directly related to his church or his faith.

While he is a strong proponent of donating 10 percent, he says that we have to analyze how we spend the other 90 percent of our money to maximize our positive impact on our society.

For instance, say someone gave away 10 percent of her income to charities. Yet she spent another 10 percent of her income for shoes that sit in the back of her closet. How we spend our money, where we spend it, and on what, can contribute to a healthier and more just society. So we encourage you to regularly examine where you spend your money. You may discover that cutting back in certain spending areas allows you to afford healthier food, lets you avoid feeling guilty about certain purchases, and may even bring more meaning to your life.

LIVING A SIMPLER LIFE

If somebody gave you the option to live a simpler life, you'd probably think, "That's great, but I can't do it." We suggest that you examine your assumptions as to why you can't. There are probably a couple of reasons—time and money. But are these valid reasons?

Consider what is really important and valuable in your life, and write down your priorities. Then, ask yourself the question "Do these things that I spend time and money on match my core values and desires and my vision for my life?" If they are not part of your vision—and it's likely that at least a few of them will not be—we suggest you systematically try to eliminate these items from your life.

Can you, for example, work less? Most people believe that we can get great satisfaction from our work, and the ideal, of course, is to have a meaningful job. But you can have a meaningful, satisfying job and still work fewer hours at it. It might even make the job better! You could also find that the economic cost is much less than you think it would be, and that there are many benefits to working less. For example, you'll reduce your commuting expenses, you'll need fewer business clothes, and you'll have more time to cook instead of ordering out.

Many people in two-working-person households are barely able to make the payments on their many possessions. The issue here is not how much people work but how much they consume. When you reduce your consumption, you can reduce your stress, the pressure in your life, and even your fears.

The problem is that most people don't want to live a simpler life. They don't want to give up material possessions. In fact, most people want a lot more.

We realize it's not easy to cut back to part-time work or to stop working altogether. It can involve very difficult and complicated decisions. But remember the words of Socrates: "The unexamined life is not worth living." If you examine what is really important in your life and how you want to be spending your time, you may discover that material possessions aren't that important after all.

If you want to explore the idea of living more simply, Jerome M. Segal's *Graceful Simplicity: The Philosophy and Politics of the Alternative American Dream* and *Your Money or Your Life: Trans-*

forming Your Relationship with Money and Achieving Financial Independence by Joe Dominguez and Vicki Robin are two books that show you how to change your life so you'll need less money, thus allowing you more flexibility in how you spend your time.

TITHING

Tithing, as we have noted, is making a commitment to give 10 percent of your income away. We believe there are actually four types of tithing:

- *Money tithing.* Give away one-tenth of your income each year. The easiest way to reach this target is to consume less and live more simply.
- *Time tithing.* Devote 10 percent of your waking time to others or to causes. This is probably the second-best-known form of tithing.
- *Idea tithing.* This concept, developed by author Mark Victor Hansen, calls for you to share 10 percent of your good ideas with others, with no expectation of return.
- *Intrapersonal tithing.* A concept Harvey developed, which involves committing time to improve yourself.

Money Tithing

Most of the world's religions promote tithing, and statistics show that people of strong faith give away a larger percentage of their income than the nonreligious. This might be linked to a stronger sense of community or to religions promoting the giving of 10 percent of your income to your faith group.

However, you don't have to be religious to be a generous giver. In the United States last year, 6 percent of the population tithed, according to *Harper's* magazine. Many individuals who are not wealthy give much more than 10 percent of their income.

If everyone tithed, the generosity would make an incredible difference in reducing social problems. Organizations that solve human problems would have about four to ten times their current level of support. People wouldn't be turned away from shelters, hospices would have enough beds, and children with learning disabilities would get the help they need. The benefits to all of us would be tremendous.

Can you be a good giver without tithing? Absolutely. We just think it's a great goal to aspire to and one that will increase the positive impact you will make on the lives of others.

Time Tithing

Time is perhaps even more valuable than money. Can you devote 10 percent of your free time to volunteer work? Each of us has probably thirty to fifty hours a week when we can choose what to do. Often we spend this time watching TV, surfing the Internet, or shopping. Could you free up three to five hours a week to do volunteer work?

We realize that many people are in situations where this is not possible—commutes are longer, you could be breastfeeding an infant who doesn't sleep enough, you may have to work two jobs to feed your family. We only ask you to carefully evaluate your time and decide if you can do a little bit more. Can you be more efficient or effective in how you allocate your time? Can you reduce your TV watching, Web surfing, or shopping time? Can you get more exercise so you have the energy to give to others?

It's important to look at your volunteer time over a longer period. You may sit on a board that requires three weekend meetings a year. That banks a lot of time.

Consider mentoring, counseling a friend in crisis, or helping with homework as volunteer time. Even giving your spouse or children massages can be included. All help counts. You are giving of yourself, you aren't paid, and you are helping another human being in need. You are also helping yourself. We believe that time allocated to kind acts gives us energy, boosts our immune system, and releases those positive chemicals called endorphins.

People already do a lot of volunteer work. Approximately 20 billion volunteer hours are donated to community organizations in the United States each year.

Idea Tithing

Idea tithing is similar to all other forms of tithing. Simply, it involves donating 10 percent of your ideas, intellectual efforts, or creative concepts so that others benefit.

Idea tithing is inexpensive to you but potentially bountiful to others. Moreover, when you start sharing ideas with others, you generate many more ideas yourself. And you expand your giving muscles.

Mark Victor Hansen, who came up with the concept of idea tithing, has written *The Miracle of Tithing*, which you can download from his Web site (see the resource list). He has two rules for idea tithing:

1. Everyone can generate a good idea.
2. Give without expectation of return.

While money is necessary to improve our world, ideas are at least as important. That's one reason why Paul Brainerd, former ALDUS Corporation president, decided to form a new group to link professionals and nonprofits. Brainerd's vision was to get professionals to invest their time, skills, resources, and ideas to make a difference. He and other technology industry leaders formed Social Venture Partners (SVP).

SVP was started in Seattle, and satellite groups are being created across the world. The founders' vision was to build an organization that uses a venture capital model to help nonprofits. The "partners" protect their investment in good causes by also offering contacts and ideas. The consequence is the partners bring fresh ideas, new skills, and other resources to hundreds of social causes. SVP members acknowledge that they get as much back emotionally as they give in time, ideas, and resources.

Intrapersonal Tithing

You can't give what you don't have. If you are physically, emotionally, and spiritually drained, you have little to give. You can give more effectively when you lead a balanced life and take care of yourself. As comedian Lily Tomlin says, "For fast-acting relief, try slowing down."

Harvey's concept of intrapersonal tithing suggests that you devote 10 percent of your time to becoming a better, healthier, and wiser individual.

There are 8,760 hours in your year. The average person sleeps eight hours a day, or 2,920 hours. That leaves 5,840 waking hours. After you subtract other essential commitments, such as:

- work—40 hours × 50 = 2,000 hours,
- buying, preparing, and eating food—2 hours × 365 days = 730 hours,
- performing toiletries, cleaning clothes, etc.—about 200 hours, and
- commuting—about 300 hours,

you have 2,610 hours left.

Each of us has unique and compelling claims on this leftover time. Helping a child with homework, family get-togethers, or a special hobby can take hundreds of additional hours from your "spare" time.

For the purposes of this chapter, however, let's estimate that you have approximately 2,000 hours each year that are somewhat flexible. Ten percent of this would be 200 hours. We encourage you to take at least this much time to tithe to yourself. Ideally, you could even consider 10 percent of your waking time, or 584 hours.

Two hundred hours is just about 4 hours per week; 584 hours works out to 11 hours, 14 minutes, a week. Within this range, consider committing time to some of the following activities. Each of them will enhance your personal growth and your ability to give to others.

- Read fiction and nonfiction to inspire yourself.
- Read books that teach you new skills and knowledge.
- Read books that stimulate you to look at the world in a different way.

- Spend time in nature. Research shows that contact with nature makes people happier, and you will place a higher value on nature.
- Commit to exercising at least three times a week.
- Do yoga.
- Meditate or pray.
- Spend time with your loved ones.
- Consider therapy if you have unresolved issues that cause you pain or that have a negative impact on your life.
- Learn to listen to others.
- Walk.
- Laugh.

When you enhance your knowledge, learn new ideas, and gain new skills, you have much more to offer others. Greater knowledge can lead to better jobs, higher income, and more personal satisfaction.

When you give time to yourself in the ways we list above, you'll enhance your health. Exercise will give you more energy. You'll feel better and protect yourself against disease and injuries. You'll have more enthusiasm, and you'll work harder. When you eat well, you can live longer and have more resistance to disease. When you practice yoga, you gain flexibility and strengthen your body. Each of these activities represents a form of personal giving.

When you nurture your spirit through prayer or meditation or by spending time in nature, you become a more compassionate person. You are more likely to have healthier relationships, a positive attitude to life, and a feeling of abundance. By intrapersonal tithing you make a time commitment to your growth and health—and you'll have much more to share with others.

ESCALATOR GIVING

As we mentioned previously, almost every religion has a tradition of tithing. However, many people find giving 10 percent daunting, and statistics show the vast majority of North Americans give only between half of 1 percent and 2 percent to nonprofits or religious groups each year.

Increasing your giving from 1 percent of your annual income to 10 percent means you would give away ten times as much. Emotionally, this leap is difficult for most people to make, so we have a suggestion for you to consider. Harvey developed a concept called Escalator Giving, which we believe will help you increase your giving while barely noticing the impact on your finances. There are two strategies that make Escalator Giving easier.

> STRATEGY 1: Escalator giving means increasing what you give by 1 percent each year until you reach 10 percent. We call it escalator giving because it's easy, smooth, and your giving goes up. So if you gave 2 percent last year, try 3 percent this year. You may find this so easy that you'll start adding 2 percent a year until you reach your target. You'll be surprised at how generous you are and how easy it is. Soon you are at a much higher level of giving, and you'll be happier to be there.
> STRATEGY 2: Another strategy to make it easier for you to give more is to start making automatic monthly pledges

(weekly or biweekly, if you prefer). Monthly pledges are a convenient way for donors to give (they don't have to remember to mail in a donation and can plan their giving for the year). Monthly gifts given by credit card or automatic bank transfer are inexpensive for charities because they save processing costs. This means more of a donor's gift will go to an organization's mission.

You decide how much and to whom you want to give. You might plan to give $30 a month (or $1 a day) to a cause. Then you authorize the nonprofit to receive a fixed monthly amount, which is transferred from your bank account or credit card, or deducted from your paycheck, and deposited in the organization's bank account.

Over the years, hundreds of people have told Harvey that they have not missed this money. We believe you will not miss it either. At the end of the year, you'll receive a tax receipt and will be surprised to see how much you've accomplished. It's a wonderful and convenient way to help nonprofits.

The principle behind monthly giving is similar to the concept of paying yourself first. That is, you set aside 10 percent of your income as savings for your future. Then you deduct another 10 percent to be donated to good causes. You live on the rest. The process works at every income level.

If you think it's hard to save or give money away when you have a low income, consider the example of Oseola McCarthy. Oseola saved most of what little she made from washing and ironing people's clothes, and in 1995, at the age of eighty-seven, she donated $150,000 to the University of Southern Mississippi for student scholarships.

If you work for a nonprofit or are a donor and you think these pledges are too small to bother with, think again. Many organizations raise tens of millions of dollars through pledges. Many nonprofits in Europe solicit only monthly pledges. A number of the groups Harvey works with earn 25 to 50 percent of their income from monthly pledges. Everyone benefits from this simple pledge system.

PLANNED GIVING

Most people make their gift-giving decisions when prompted. They get a call, a letter, or are asked personally to give. Relatively little giving is planned, with two exceptions. The first is monthly giving, described above. The second is the field of legacies or bequests, annuities, opening an "advised fund" at a community or public foundation, or establishing a private foundation. These are situations where you may need both financial and legal advice to maximize your giving.

Both monthly giving and bequests allow you to act in accordance with your values. They allow you to give strategically, rather then just reacting to the prompting of a letter or a personal request.

Thinking about where your priorities lie does require more time and effort on your part. However, you will find you enjoy the involvement and you'll feel your gifts are more effective.

GIVING FOR THE BIG PICTURE

Whether you decide to tithe time, money, or ideas, we urge you to set aside a portion of your giving for the "big picture." Private generosity is extremely important. However, it won't solve all the problems at a time when governments make financial decisions that hurt many people.

Let's take one powerful example. In the USA, the George W. Bush administration implemented tax cuts that transferred $100 billion a year to the wealthiest Americans (despite protests from some of the richest people in the country). At the same time, his government cut low-income child care, health care, literacy programs, energy assistance, and many other programs designed to protect the poor and vulnerable. It will take common action to reverse or prevent government decisions like this or similar ones, here or in other countries.

One-on-one efforts are important, but if that's all people do, it's too easy for men and women with power to make choices that damage everyone. That's why it's so important to pay attention to what governments and organizations do and to challenge them when they violate what you believe is just. We can't withdraw from our common responsibilities. That's the price we pay for living in a democracy.

Similarly, it is important for all of us to "live lightly on the earth." When people consume less, recycle, take mass transit, bicycle, or drive fuel-efficient cars, they make a contribution to a cleaner environment. These are wonderful actions, but individuals must also convince major corporations and elected leaders to act in ways that respect the earth.

Again, this requires a big-picture view and big-picture actions. You don't have to make these actions the sum total of your contributions. But you want to reserve some resources for them because that's how major change will occur. And this can be a great way to maximize the return on your time or money investment.

Working on the big picture is not easy, but it is essential, and it is where giving takes on a new dimension.

The core issues that cause injustice or the growing gap between the rich and the poor are complicated and difficult to resolve, but that doesn't mean you should ignore them. When you work on these issues, you must be prepared to meet resistance; there will always be vested interests that benefit from the status quo. As Dom Hélder Pessoa Câmara, a Brazilian priest who worked with his country's poorest people, said, "When I gave food to the poor, they called me saint. When I asked why the poor were hungry, they called me a communist." Even people who derive no particular benefit from the status quo will often resist change because generally people don't like change, even though it can be positive.

When you act to protect the environment, you'll also meet resistance. Almost every time the environment is damaged, whether through overfishing, clear-cutting ancient forests, or dumping toxins in drinking water, a few people profit and they don't want to change.

Fighting racism or sexism is hard because people grow up with entrenched ideas, stereotypes, and cultural conditions that promote discrimination against others. Often it is in the interests of powerful groups or individuals to ensure that racism or sexism divides people who might otherwise come together to challenge wealth or power.

Where is giving in all this?

Front and center.

We encourage you to give money, time, and energy to individuals or organizations that tackle the root causes of social problems. This, in effect, leverages your giving. You are then devoting some of your time, talents, gifts, or attention to the big picture.

Tracy Gary and Melissa Kohner, authors of *Inspired Philanthropy*, wrote: "Giving of your time and money is more than simply doing good. It is a conscious, intentional act to weave oneself into a caring culture." As you give time and money to do good, you strengthen the social fabric of your community, which extends to the four corners of the world. Every act is a strand in weaving a cloth of strength, comfort, care, and love.

key points

It is better to give than not give. However, how and what you offer can give your gift a greater impact.

You have enormous capacity to give.
Give wholeheartedly.
Give of yourself, not just your possessions.
Give with respect, humility, and compassion.
Give unconditionally.
Give even in hardship. There are other things to give
    besides money.
Consider tithing—money, time, ideas, or intrapersonally.
Consider escalator giving.
Be balanced in your approach to giving and to life.

CHAPTER 5

corporate giving

Giving is not just for individuals. Most of us work for businesses or organizations that can also give back to our communities. When we promote giving in these organizations, we can influence other people, make a difference to the communities we live in, and create positive change. Therefore, many of the benefits that we talk about in this book also apply to corporations, albeit in different ways. And like personal giving, corporate giving, when done with service in mind as opposed to trying to get something back, has many benefits. People want to work for businesses that are seen to be good corporate citizens. Corporate giving helps attract employees with values to such businesses and it helps to keep them.

This chapter about corporate giving may not directly relate to you if you are not part of a corporation. However, the principles of giving back, whether to customers, employees, or the environment, will be useful to you whatever organization or institution you belong to. These principles apply to co-ops, trade unions, service clubs, even online networks.

Corporations are almost always formed to create profits. Their mandate is not to give. However, surprising as it may sound, giving is still one of the key ingredients of corporate success.

If you work for a business, ask yourself the following questions:

Is your organization optimizing customer or client growth?

Do you know what attracts customers or clients to do business with you?

Do you attract and retain talented employees?

Has your corporation established trust and credibility in the marketplace?

Is your company socially responsible?

Upon reflecting on these questions you will realize the importance of giving to customers, employees, the community, and the environment.

giving to customers

The foundation of any business is giving to its customers. Looking after their needs, solving their problems, keeping them happy is all part of the giving to customers that creates loyalty, repeat business, and word-of-mouth recommendations.

Enterprise Rent-a-Car grew from a small leasing company in Missouri into a $9 billion global powerhouse. Their motto was to keep customers not just satisfied but completely satisfied! Their eight-step strategy was

- Actively listen.
- Record what the customer says.
- Apologize.
- Find out what the customer wants.
- Propose a solution.
- If the customer does not like the solution, ask him or her for the reasons.
- Follow up and ensure that the customer has been satisfied.
- Let the customer save face.

The outcome of following these recommendations is a completely satisfied customer. If you look at each of the eight steps, you'll see that there is an element of giving to the customer—be it the gift of listening, attention, or solution.

Thomas Edison, the founder of General Electric, said, "I never perfected an invention that I did not think in terms of service it might give to others." Without the service/giving element, not much can be achieved with the customers.

Walt Disney's mission was "to bring a smile to a child's face," and he was able to persevere through a lot of struggles and challenges to make his dream a reality. Of course, there was a profit motive—all corporations have that—but notice the link to giving: bringing a smile to a child's face.

Curves, which is now the largest fitness franchise in the world, built its success by developing clear, simple, user-friendly workouts that busy women could complete quickly. They put the customer first, and now they are first!

An individual working in a corporation can also take the initiative to give to his or her customer, irrespective of position held. In October 2007 Azim missed his connecting flight to Dar-es-Salaam from Johannesburg. He could not get another flight until the next morning. As he was looking for a place to book hotels, he bumped into a woman who looked like she worked at the airport. Azim told her what he was looking for, and she went out of her way and spent twenty minutes with him to find him a hotel, a driver for a tour, and a ride back the next morning. And guess what, Azim later found out that this was not even in her job description. She took the initiative and did her colleague's job. We all get chances to go the extra mile and give help to our customers.

Sometimes when you have much on your plate and you need someone to give to you, it is hard to give. But if you lighten up and give even a smile, you will feel better. Azim was doing a seminar for a leading bank in India that employed twelve thousand people when someone asked him the question: How do I give and be kind when I have already done that for twelve hours and yet another customer comes in?

Azim replied: "You have two choices of how to treat the customer—either with a frown or a smile. A smile requires you to use three muscles, while a frown requires sixty-three. You decide: How many muscles do you want to use when you are tired?"

giving to employees

It is becoming harder to find and retain talented employees. Harnessing the potential of employees is also crucial, since they are the most important asset any company has. To attract and retain good employees requires a giving culture. Looking after their needs and providing an enabling environment that fosters learning, growth, and contribution is part and parcel of that giving.

The phenomenal growth of Starbucks has rested partly on its philosophy of treating its employees as partners and offering its customers a special experience each time they visit their coffee shop. Starbucks is known to open stores early to let a customer in and has even set up tables at train stations to offer free coffee. These practices are grounded in the principle of service and giving. And it's also smart business practice.

Robert Greenleaf first coined the term *Servant Leadership* in 1970, and it has been widely used since. It implies a leader who is a giver. One who sees the richness of others, facilitates their growth and potential. A servant leader is less of a boss and more of a partner. In their book *Firms of Endearment*, Rajendra S. Sisodia, David B. Wolfe, and Jagdish N. Sheth show that companies from Costco to Wegmens are working to become the ultimate value creators, generating every form of value that matters: emotional, experiential, social, and financial. Part of the organizational vision of these firms is a dedication to servant leadership. These firms have done eight times better in terms of return on investment as compared to the S&P 500 firms for a ten-year period ending June 30, 2006.

Part of Servant Leadership is showing respect to your colleagues. One of Azim's participants at a two-day event for senior corporate executives was sharing a situation in which he had replaced a supervisor who was demoted to another position in the same team. The participant was sharing his frustration at not only not getting cooperation from his predecessor but also having the whole team support the old leader. Another participant shared a similar situation but with a positive outcome. This other participant said that when she realized what was happening, she was extra careful in terms of making sure that the old leader "saved face" among his peers. She did that by showing tremendous respect to the previous leader, involving him in key decisions, and seeking guidance from him in front of his peers. This approach of showing respect not only prevented employees from taking sides but also resulted in securing the old leader's help and cooperation in carrying out the new leader's tasks. Giving respect and allowing the old leader to save face created a favorable outcome for all concerned.

In a research of two hundred high-potential leaders around the world (those who could jump at a moment's notice to better-paying positions elsewhere) Marshall Goldsmith and Mark Reiter in their book *What Got You Here Won't Get You There* reveal that what kept the employees loyal was meaningful work, camaraderie, community feeling, and pursuing part of their calling—not a paycheck.

The ultimate for any organization is to have the employees see their work as a calling—to create enormous success for all stockholders and make a positive difference to worthwhile causes.

Companies such as UPS, Hewlett Packard, and Starbucks, which have had some sort of employee ownership either by way of a stock purchase plan or stock options, have seen great growth in their business. Giving a piece of the pie to their employees has paid off.

By the time you read this book, a company we mention might have gone off the rails. Perhaps they lost their focus on service and giving, perhaps they overextended themselves, or perhaps global competition has damaged them. The point is, though, that those companies that have embraced service and giving have outshone their competitors. They are better positioned to withstand economic turmoil. It's good business to care. And it's better for the communities in which these businesses work.

giving to the community

Every corporation operates within a community. Corporations that give to the community benefit from its support. The giving creates trust and credibility. It reflects good citizenship.

Harvey's family decided to sign up with SPUD, a local organics door-to-door delivery service. They started off getting a box of greens that were produced by local farmers, thereby cutting the miles traveled from farm to table and reducing greenhouse gas emissions. Then they ordered a lot of the other healthy food options SPUD offered, saving time and supporting corporations that are environmentally conscious. These were good reasons to sign up for the weekly service. Then Harvey learned more—about how SPUD supported local farmers, how they were very generous to food banks and other social service organizations in many different ways. So a few years later, Harvey decided to become a small investor to help support SPUD's growth. Their mission and service reflected his values. Later, he was invited to join their board of advisers—essentially a volunteer task because he loves what they do.

So by being a good corporate citizen, SPUD attracted Harvey's investment and his business skills. And he's not alone. Many experienced business leaders have helped SPUD in similar ways. Today, it is by far the largest organics home delivery company in North America, stretching from California to Alberta. Its founder and CEO David Van Seters had a dream: to help promote local, organic food. To help the communities where they operate. To treat staff and customers with respect and care. He's done a great job based on values, and the value of his company has grown tremendously as a result.

Stephen M. R. Covey and Rebecca R. Merrill in their wonderful book *The Speed of Trust* talk about the speed at which work gets done where there is a foundation of trust. They refer to five waves of trust—self, relationship, organization, market, and societal trust, which are built around credibility, consistent behavior, alignment, reputation, and contribution. Again, within all these waves there is an element of giving either to self, colleague, customer, or community.

Trust is won as you build confidence in the market by your consistency and giving nature.

GIVING TO THE ENVIRONMENT

Today, any company that ignores the need to be environmentally friendly is looked down upon by the market. Millions of potential investors will avoid these companies, and some of them may face huge potential liabilities. In addition, these companies lose out on savings that could materialize from be-

ing prudent in using their resources. Both individuals and corporations can play a part in leaving the world a better place
than they found it.

IKEA, for instance, uses flat packaging, which squeezes every
millimeter of use out of every box. This enables the company to
pack its trains and trucks tighter. The packaging saves up to 15
percent on fuel cost per item while also reducing the number of
trees cut down.

Xerox saved $2 million over ten years from its waste-saving
program, serving the environment as well as their bottom line.

The Body Shop was sold for $1.14 billion in 2006. Its value
was enhanced by its great mix of social consciousness and business
practice. The founder, Anita Roddick, was a strong proponent of
human rights, environmental, and other worthwhile causes.

Here are just some of the ways Harvey's company demonstrates day-to-day environmental commitment:

- At least 97 percent of their direct-mail pieces are
  printed on FSC-certified paper and envelopes. This
  means that the paper comes from well-managed forests and recycled sources.
- For all in-office everyday printing, they use Harbour
  100 paper, which is 100 percent post-consumer recycled, chlorine free, Green-E, and FSC-certified.
- Through an internal recycling program, they diverted
  65 cubic yards of recyclable materials from landfills
  last year alone.
- All of their old monitors and computers are either
  donated to charities or picked up for recycling—they
  never go into the Dumpster.

• Every year they participate in the Commuter Challenge organized by BEST (Better Environmentally Sound Transportation). Many of the staff cycle to work regularly, even from long distances. That keeps staff healthy, and they are all very proud to have finished in first place for 100 percent participation in a number of years.

All companies, small or big, can participate in making an impact on the environment. And staff will feel good about doing this. And environmental campaigns don't have to be organized from the top down. Any employee can take responsibility for initiating an internal campaign.

Rosabeth Moss Kanter recently returned from a Harvard Business Study with a research team inside a dozen global giants, including IBM, Procter & Gamble, Omron, CEMEX, Cisco, and Banco Real, to discover what has been driving change. After conducting more than three hundred fifty interviews on five continents, Kanter came away with a strong sense that we are witnessing the dawn of a new model of corporate power. There is a stress on openness, inclusion, and making the world a better place. Companies have become as creative and nimble as much smaller ones even while taking on social and environmental challenges of a scale that only large enterprises could attempt.

In 2008 Google donated $30 million in new grants and investments. They plan to focus a massive philanthropic endeavor on erasing the usual boundaries between the for-profit and non-profit worlds. The first set of major five-to-eight-year initiatives includes efforts to create systems to:

- help predict and prevent disease pandemics,
- empower the poor with information about public services, and
- create jobs by investing in small and midsize businesses in the developing world.

The assets currently set aside for the company's philanthropic arm, Google.org are valued at about $2 billion.

GIVING FROM THE BOTTOM UP

In a business, the majority of "giving" projects are not enlisted by the CEO or senior management; they are by individuals in a wide variety of positions. And, in fact, even if giving projects are developed by the CEO, they become successful only with the passion and energy of other staff.

Each December Amnesty International celebrates Human Rights Day with a global letter-writing campaign called Write for Rights; the campaign has generated millions of letters to help free individuals who are persecuted and often tortured for their beliefs.

This past year Harvey's executive assistant, Carla Voss, launched what will become an annual commitment for the company: getting staff together and writing letters for Human Rights Day. Carla spent considerable energy to find powerful stories of people abused by their own governments and got all of the staff excited about being part of a global movement to save people from torture.

Anyone can initiate a Write for Rights campaign in their workplace. This type of giving action builds a team. It helps to connect you to individuals halfway around the world. And these letter campaigns have helped free many prisoners and save many lives.

All the above examples refer to a blend between "corporate" and "giving." Azim has coined the term Corporate Sufi™, which reflects this blend: *corporate* symbolizing success, power, ambition, and material abundance; *Sufi* symbolizing the essence, principles, giving, and spiritual abundance.* When corporate executives display these traits, they have a potential not only for material abundance but also for spiritual abundance.

The burning desire of the power to give is inside all of us. As you give, you get. It creates a win for both the giver and the recipient. And therein lies the power of giving!

key points

Corporate giving

- optimizes customer and client growth
- attracts and helps retain talented employees
- enhances credibility and trust
- makes the company socially responsible
- benefits all stockholders

---

*The word *Sufi* comes from the Arabic word *Soof,* which literally means "wool." It was the material from which simple robes of the early Muslim mystics were made. It symbolizes humility, simplicity, and purity.

giving up

Do you want to find more meaning, fulfillment, and abundance in your life? Try giving. Also, try giving up.

In our fast-paced society we can get into an activity trap in which we are busy for the sake of being busy. Giving up nonessential items in our life can help us give more.

We've compiled four lists of things you might consider giving up. These lists are by no means comprehensive. And the items in the lists are not necessarily bad or harmful to you. However, moderation is the key. If you reduce or eliminate the time and money you spend in these areas, you may feel better, physically or emotionally. You'll be able to reallocate your resources, for your own good and the good of others.

When you go through these lists, pick two or three items in each group that may be a problem for you.

Group 1. Would your friends and acquaintances think you have a problem in these areas?

- sloth
- envy
- anger
- avarice
- greed
- lust
- gossip
- hatred
- fear

Group 2. Would your friends and acquaintances think you have a problem in these areas?

- drugs
- alcohol
- gambling
- prescription drugs
- smoking
- workaholism
- fundamentalism
- intolerance
- bias against other races, religions, or cultures

Group 3. Do you spend a lot of time watching, using, thinking about, or consuming these?

- TV
- Internet
- sports events
- shopping
- motor vehicles
- unhealthy food

Group 4. Would you like to give up your

- prejudices
- pain
- judgmentalism
- procrastination
- littering

We encourage you to spend some energy on the particular areas you've checked off. Imagine how great you'll feel once you have them under control.

Make a commitment to action. Remember: To give to others, you have to give to yourself. If your life and priorities aren't balanced, you have less to give and are less likely to reach your full potential. Are we saying you need to be perfect in all areas? No. We simply believe that all of us are happier when we strive to be better people. We also believe perfection is impossible. But progress *is* possible and healthy.

a final word

Giving is a beautiful experience. By practicing giving, you make a difference to others and to yourself. It is a powerful feeling to be able to give regularly.

By giving, you can live to your potential, avoid loneliness, become fearless, touch your spirit, and find meaning and fulfillment. The universe is abundant. As Azim says, "The more you are in the flow of giving, the more abundance flows through you."

There is no shortage of people and places you can give to. You can give to yourself, your family, your elders, your children, your community, nonprofit social organizations, and the planet.

You can give the next generation many gifts. One of the best gifts you can give children is to teach them the beauty of giving. You can also teach them how to take care of the environment so that they leave it in better condition for future generations.

Everyone can give something—a smile, a prayer, a good thought. Giving can be tangible or intangible. You can give wisdom, love, laughter, time, money, skills, attention, or forgiveness.

It is not only what you give that matters but also how you give it. When you give unconditionally and with respect, you create the biggest impact.

It is good to give when things are going great, but you can also give in hardship. Sometimes, by giving in hardship you forget your problems, create breakthroughs, and find solutions to your challenges.

You can give a little or you can give a lot. It is your choice. The more you give, the more you receive. Your rewards may be instantaneous or they may take a while, but no giving goes unnoticed by the universal laws of nature.

By living a simple life and applying the discipline of tithing from a young age, you can create a habit of giving that becomes as natural as breathing.

You can also work to give up some of the bad habits that stop your progress and dampen your giving capacity, such as watching too much television, smoking, using drugs, or drinking too much.

WILL YOU HELP?

Will you take a few minutes or a few hours to help promote the power of giving?

Our hope is that this book will inspire you to become a better and more compassionate giver. We believe giving will add more meaning to your life and help build healthier communities everywhere. If you believe in the power of giving, we'd like you to consider doing three things that will spread the word:

- Tell your friends about this book and encourage them to read it.
- Make a personal commitment to becoming a conscious giver.
- Become a Power Giver: promote the ideas contained in this book.

We hope you have enjoyed our book and have been inspired to continue your giving and making a difference. We hope that you find abundance, happiness, and inspiration from *The Power of Giving!*

Thank you,
Azim and Harvey

key points

Give up

- envy, anger, and fear
- undesirable social habits: drugs, smoking, and alcohol
- too much TV
- intolerance, workaholism, fundamentalism
- prejudices and judgmentalism

Resource List

Introduction

Make-a-Wish Foundation: www.wish.org; www.makeawish.ca

Azim Jamal's Web site: www.azimjamal.com

Harvey McKinnon's Web site: www.harveymckinnon.com

The Tipping Point: How Little Things Can Make a Big Difference by Malcolm Gladwell is available at www.gladwell.com.

Chapter One: Why Give?

To learn more about Abraham Maslow's theories of self-actualization and the hierarchy of human needs, read *Toward a Psychology of Being* by Abraham Maslow (John W. Wiley & Sons, 1998). For a listing of books and articles by and about Abraham Maslow, visit www.maslow.com.

To learn more about the Princess Margaret Hospital Foundation and the inspiring "Wings of Hope" display, please visit www. pmhf-uhn.ca.

Bowling Alone: The Collapse and Revival of American Community by Robert Putnam, with Don Cohen and Lewis Feldstein. Simon & Schuster, 2000.

Chapter Two: What Can You Give?

Visit www.payitforward.warnerbros.com/Pay_It_Forward to read about how Pay It Forward got started.

LAUGHS (Laughing at and Understanding Good Humor Seminars): www.laughsrus.com

For more information on the Power of Hope go to: www. powerofhope.org.

Living Donors Online: www.livingdonorsonline.org

United Network for Organ Sharing: www.unos.org

Canadian Blood Services: www.bloodservices.ca

American Association of Blood Banks: www.aabb.org/

To find out more about touch research, visit the Web site of the Touch Research Institutes (TRI), founded in 1992 by Dr. Tiffany Field: www.miami.edu/touch-research/

Anger: Wisdom for Cooling the Flames by Thich Nhat Hanh. Riverhead Books, 2001.

Survival Is Not Enough: Why Smart Companies Abandon Worry and Embrace Change by Seth Godin. The Free Press, 2002.

Building Moral Intelligence: The Seven Essential Virtues That Teach Kids to Do the Right Thing by Michele Borba. Jossey-Bass, 2001.

When the Body Says No: Understanding the Stress-Disease Connection by Dr. Gabor Maté. John Wiley & Sons, Inc., 2003.

Who Dies? An Investigation of Conscious Living and Conscious Dying by Stephen and Ondrea Levine. Anchor Books, 1989.

Love Is the Killer App: How to Win Business and Influence Friends by Tim Sanders. Three Rivers Press, 2002.

Leadership from Within by Peter Urs Bender. The Achievement Group, 2002.

Seven Steps to Lasting Happiness by Azim Jamal. Jaico Publishing House, 2007.

The Soul of Money by Lynne Twist. W. W. Norton & Company, 2003.

You Just Don't Understand: Women and Men in Conversation by Deborah Tannen. Ballantine Books, 1991.

The 7 Habits of Highly Effective People by Stephen R. Covey. Fireside, 1990.

Chapter Three: To Whom Should You Give?

You may want to look at a few of the books on meditation that we have listed on our Web site (www.thepowerofgiving.org/resources).

There are many resources that can help you improve your relationships and your perception of the world. We list a number of them on our Web site: www.thepowerofgiving.org/resources.

Learn more about John Gottman and The Gottman Institute at www.gottman.com.

Conscious Loving: The Journey to Co-Commitment by Gay and Kathlyn Hendricks. Bantam, 1992.

To learn more about the project Learning to Give, visit: www.learningtogive.org.

Non-Smokers' Rights Association: www.nsra-adnf.ca.

For more information on the International Kids Fund, visit their Web site: www.internationalkidsfund.org.

David Suzuki started the foundation that bears his name: www.davidsuzuki.org.

The full text of Severn Suzuki's 1993 speech at the Kyoto Global Forum is available at www.sloth.gr.jp/Severn-Espeech93.htm. Search for "Severn Suzuki" at youtube.com to find a short video clip of her speaking.

A Web site that evaluates charities in the United States: www.charitynavigator.org.

Soul of a Citizen: Living with Conviction in a Cynical Time by Paul Rogat Loeb. St. Martin's Griffin, 1999.

Building Moral Intelligence: The Seven Essential Virtues That Teach Kids to Do the Right Thing by Michele Borba. Jossey-Bass, 2001.

A Good Life by Al Etmanski. Planned Lifetime Advocacy Network (PLAN), 2000.

Chapter Four: How, When, Where, and How Much to Give

To find out more about giving, please visit www.thepowerofgiving.org.

To get more information on monthly giving, visit Harvey's Web site at www.harveymckinnon.com/services/monthly_giving.html.

Graceful Simplicity: The Philosophy and Politics of the Alternative American Dream by Jerome M. Segal. Henry Holt and Company, 1999.

Your Money or Your Life: Transforming Your Relationship with Money and Achieving Financial Independence by Joe Dominguez and Vicki Robin. Penguin Books, 1999.

Inspired Philanthropy by Tracy Gary and Melissa Kohner. Jossey-Bass, 2002.

The Miracle of Tithing by Mark Victor Hansen is downloadable from: www.markvictorhansen.com/idea_tithing.pdf.

Chapter Five: Corporate Giving

Firms of Endearment by Rajendra S. Sisodia, David B. Wolfe, and Jagdish N. Sheth. Wharton School Publishing, 2007.

What Got You Here Won't Get You There by Marshall Goldsmith and Mark Reiter. Hyperion 2007.

www.spud.ca, www.spud.com

The Speed of Trust: The One Thing That Changes Everything by Stephen M. R. Covey and Rebecca Merrill. Free Press, 2008.

Other Helpful and Inspiring Books About Giving and Volunteering

The Impossible Will Take a Little While: A Citizen's Guide to Hope in a Time of Fear by Paul Rogat Loeb. Basic Books, 2004.

Greenpeace: How a Group of Ecologists, Journalists, and Visionaries Changed the World by Rex Weyler. Raincoast, 2004.

Transforming the Mind: Teachings on Generating Compassion by His Holiness the Dalai Lama. Thorsons, 2000.

How to Change the World: Social Entrepreneurs and the Power of New Ideas by David Bornstein. Oxford University Press, 2004.

How Can I Help? Stories and Reflections on Service by Ram Dass and Paul Gorman. Alfred A. Knopf, 1985.

A Pace of Grace by Linda Kavelin Popov. Plume, 2004.

Fire in the Soul: A New Psychology of Spiritual Optimism by Joan Borysenko. Warner Books, 1993.

The Power of Kindness: The Unexpected Benefits of Leading a

Compassionate Life by Piero Ferrucci. Trans. by Vivien Ferrucci. Tarcher/Penguin, 2006.

A Few More Good Causes to Consider

Free the Children: www.metowe.org

The Marmot Recovery Foundation: www.marmots.org

Earthworks: www.earthworksaction.org

The Canadian Parks and Wilderness Society: www.cpaws.org

Amnesty International: www.amnesty.ca. www.amnestyusa.org

Index

Action Aid, 113
Advice, 79–81
    body language in, 80–81
    communication in, 79–80
    feelings and, 81
Afghanistan, 113–14
Afghan refugee camp, 24
Aga Khan Foundation, The, 113
Aga Khan IV, 59
AIDS, 2, 4
Alcoholism, 59, 90
ALDUS Corporation, 148
Alternatives international development
        agency, 113
American Health, 22
Amnesty International, 167
Anderssen, Erin, 3
Anger (Hanh), 40
Anger, mindfulness and, 39
Anti-apartheid, 111

Apted, Michael, 88
Attention, to others, 77–78, 127

Balance, 82–83, 89
    exercise for, 91
Banco Real, 166
Bender, Peter Urs, 55
Benefits, of giving, 10–11, 14, 18, 19–32
    fear reduction, 21–22
    finding self, 30–32
    good health, 22–23
    living to potential, 23–24
    Maslow's hierarchy of needs and, 25–28
    meaning, fulfillment, and happiness, 28–30
    new relationships, 20
    physical, 3–4, 22–23
BEST. *See* Better Environmentally Sound
        Transportation
Better Environmentally Sound Transporta-
        tion (BEST), 166

Body Shop, The, 165
Books, for gift giving, 49–51
Borba, Michele, 49, 105
Borysenko, Joan, 87
Bowling Alone (Putnam), 21, 51, 61
Brainerd, Paul, 134, 148
Buddhism, mindfulness and, 38
*Building Moral Intelligence: The Seven
        Essential Virtues That Teach Kids to
        Do the Right Thing* (Borba), 49, 105
Burnett, Carol, 45
Bush, George W., 154
Business 2.0, 51

Câmara, Dom Hélder Pessoa, 155
Cancer, 8, 77, 115, 132
    laughter and, 46
    Princess Margaret Hospital and, 32–33
Care for others, religion promotion of, 37
Cause and effect, 31
CEMEX, 166
Children
    communication with, 101
    family giving to, 99–101
    family's teaching to give, 101–5
    feelings of, 100
    "heart fiber" of, 104–5
    laughter and, 44
    money allowance for, 102
    relationships with, 100
    time for, 100
    touch need of, 75–76
Cisco, 166
Communication. *See also* Language, body
    in advice, 79–80
    with children, 101
    of feelings, 98
Community, 105–19
    corporate giving to, 163–68
    elders in, 109–10
    global, 112–14
    Loeb research on, 108–9
    nonprofit organizations in, 114–17
    small organizations in, 117–19
    social involvement in, 19, 107–8,
        110–12
Compassion, 94–95, 102, 104–5, 129
Compromise, 95–96
*Conscious Loving: The Journey to
        Co-Commitment* (Hendricks
        and Hendricks), 94
Corporate giving, 3, 157–68

from bottom up, 167–68
to community, 163–68
to customers, 158–60
to employees, 161–63
to environment, 164–67
globally, 58
Corporate Sufi, 168
Corporation(s)
    ALDUS, 148
    Banco Real, 166
    Body Shop, The, 165
    CEMEX, 166
    Cisco, 166
    Curves, 160
    environmental protection by, 165–66
    giving by, 3, 58, 157–68
    Google, 166
    Hewlett Packard, 162
    IBM, 166
    IKEA, 165
    leadership of, 57–59
    Motorola, 58
    Omron, 166
    Procter & Gamble, 166
    Roper Center for Public Opinion survey
        on, 57–58
    social conscious policies of, 57
    Starbucks, 161, 162
    Xerox, 165
    Yahoo, 50
Covey, Stephen R., 41, 81, 98, 164
Curves, 160

Developmental disabilities, 118
Diseases
    AIDS, 2, 4
    alcoholism, 59, 90
    cancer, 8, 32–33, 46, 77, 115, 142
    kidney transplants and, 61–62
    organ donations and, 61–62
Disney, Walt, 159–60
"Doing good deeds can improve health,
        make you happier, scientists
        suggest" (Anderssen), 3
Dominguez, Joe, 145
Dove fund-raising campaign
    of Princess Margaret Hospital, 33
    van Nostrand and, 33

Edison, Thomas, 159
Education and lifelong learning, 52–53
Elders, 62–63, 109–10

in community, 109–10
 wisdom of, 54
Emerson, Ralph Waldo, 130
Enterprise Rent-a-Car, 159
Environmental protection, 119–20
 by corporations, 165–66
Escalator giving, 151–53
Exercise
 "How are you spending your time?" 64
 "How do you feel about money?" 66–67
 "How healthy are your relationships?" 99
 "The first step to helping yourself," 91
 "What new skills do you want to
  develop?" 73–74
 "Why do I want to give?" 134–35

Family, 92–93
 children, giving to, 99–101
 children, teaching to give by, 101–5
 healing relationships in, 96–99
 meetings, 101
 spouse, 93–96
 time with, 63
Fear
 leadership and, 55
 reduction, 21–22
 television watching, increase of, 21
Feeling(s), 133–35
 advice giving and, 81
 anger, 39
 of children, 100
 communication of, 98
 compassion, 94–95, 102, 104, 129
 expression of, 39–40
 fear, 21–22, 55
 forgiveness, 42–43
 in friendship, 20, 95
 fulfillment, 28–30
 giving and, 134–35
 giving up negative, 170
 grieving, 43–44
 happiness, 28–30
 "heart fiber" and, 104–5
 hope, 59–60
 humility, 128–29
 kindness, 35–36
 love, 22–23, 37–44, 95, 105
 mindfulness, 39, 87, 89
 negative, 170
 passion, 20–30
 purpose in life, 28–30
 regret, 40, 43–44

respect, 104, 127–28, 154
 of self-actualization, 25–27
 unconditional love, 38–39, 42, 105
Ferrucci, Piero, 4
Field, Tiffany, 75
Firms of Endearment (Sisodia, Wolfe, and
  Sheth), 161
First Micro Finance Bank Ltd, 69–70
Focus humanitarian agency, 24
Forgiveness, 42–43
Fried, Carol Ann, 97
Friendship, 20, 95
Fulfillment, finding of, 28–30

Galvin, Bob, 58
Gandhi, Mahatma, 24, 30
Gary, Tracy, 156
General Electric, 159
Gibran, Kahlil, 126, 127, 132
Gifts, 14, 18–19
 books as, 49–51
 relationship development through, 10
Giving. See also Benefits, of giving;
    Nonprofit organizations
 advice, 78–81
 attention, 77–78
 balance in, 82–83
 beauty of, 32–33, 172
 to community, 105–19
 compromise in, 95–96
 to family, 92–93
 fundamental human need of, 8
 globally, 1–2, 103, 112–14
 health, 75
 hope, 59–60
 how to, 14, 126–29
 items and gifts for, 14
 knowledge, 48–54
 laughter, 44–48
 leadership, 54–59
 life, 60–62
 love, 37–44
 money, 64–69
 passion in, 29–30
 physical benefits of, 3–4
 to planet, 119–22
 power of, 10–11
 receiving and, 30–31
 recipients of, 14
 rewards of, 20
 ripple effect of, 13–14
 to self, 86–91, 132–33

Giving (*continued*)
  skills, 70–74
  to spouse, 93–99
  symbiotic relationship in, 10–11
  time, 62–64
  touch, 75–77
  what you need most, 81–82
Giving, how much, 142–56
  escalator giving and, 151–53
  planned giving, 155
  private generosity and, 153–56
  simpler life and, 143–45
  tithing, 145–51
Giving, how to, 14, 126–30
  with humility, 128–29
  with respect, 127–28
  unconditionally, 129–30
Giving, reasons for, 17–34
  beautiful experience of, 32–34, 172
  benefits of, 19–32
  exercise for, 134–35
  investment return, 18–19
"Giving up," 14, 169–74
  negative attitudes, 171
  negative emotions, 170
  problem areas, 170
  sacrificing as, 38
  television, 171
Giving, when to, 130–33
  in hardship, 131–33
Giving, where to, 133–39
  emotions, values and motivations in,
    133–35
  priorities in, 138–42
  resources in, 138–39
  skills and, 135–39
Gladwell, Malcolm, 12
Global community, 112–14
Global Forum (1993), 121–22
Global giving, 1–2, 103, 112–14
Globe and Mail, 3
Godin, Seth, 49
Goldsmith, Marshall, 162
Google, 166
Gottman, John, 93
*Graceful Simplicity: The Philosophy and
    Politics of the Alternative American
    Dream* (Segal), 144
Greenleaf, Robert, 161
Grieving, 43–44

Hanh, Thich Nhat, 40

Hansen, Mark Victor, 147
Happiness, 28–30
Harper's magazine, 146
Harvard Business Study, 166
Health
  giving of, 75
  laughter and, 44
  physical benefits of giving and, 3–4,
    22–23
  volunteer work improvement on, 4, 22
"Heart fiber," compassion, order, respect,
    empathy (CORE) in, 104–5
Hendricks, Gay, 94
Hendricks, Kathlyn, 94
Hewlett Packard, 162
Hierarchy of needs, of Maslow, 25–28, *26*
Holtz Children's Hospital, 115
Honesty, 94, 95
Hope, 59–60
Hubbard, Elbert, 109
Human Rights Day, 167
Humility, 128–29
Hyde, Catherine Ryan, 36

IBM, 166
IKEA, 165
*In Darkest Hollywood: Cinema and Apart-
    heid,* McKinnon production of,
    111
Inspired Philanthropy (Gary and Kohner),
    156
Intellect and wisdom, 52–53
International Kids Fund, 115

Jackson Memorial Medical Center, 115
Jamal, Azim, 63
Journal writing, 87

Kanter, Rosabeth Moss, 166
Kidney transplants, 61–62
Kindness, 35–36
Knowledge, 48–54
  education and lifelong learning and,
    52–53
  intellect and wisdom and, 53–54
  television and, 51–52
Kohner, Melissa, 156
Krishnamurti, J., 52

Language, body, 80–81
LAUGHS Web site, 44
Laughter, 44–48

cancer and, 46
children and, 44
as medicine, 44
tragedy and, 45–47
Leadership, 54–59
corporate, 57–59
fear and, 55
qualities of, 56
volunteer work and, 55–56
Leadership from Within (Bender), 55
Learning to Give organization, 104
Levine, Ondrea, 50
Levine, Stephen, 50
Life, 60–62
organ donation and, 61–62
"Life balance," 11
Loeb, Paul, 101, 107
community research by, 108–9
Love, 37–44, 95
Christianity, Judaism, Hinduism and, 37
example of, 22–23
expression of, 42–43
making time for, 41–42
misuse of word, 40–41
sacrifice and, 38–40
unconditional, 38–39, 42, 105
Love Is the Killer App: How to Win Business and Influence Friends (Sanders), 50

Mahood, Garfield, 118
Make-A-Wish Foundation, 8–9
Mandino, Og, 31
Marx, Groucho, 51
Maslow, Abraham, hierarchy of needs of, 25–28
Massage, touch and, 76
Maté, Gabor, 49–50
McKinnon, Harvey, 111
Mead, Margaret, 112
Médecins sans Frontières (MSF), 113
Meditation, 74, 87–88, 98, 150, 156
mindfulness in, 39
on money attitude, 65–67
Mercy Corps, 113
Merrill, Rebecca R., 164
Merton, Thomas, 20
Mindfulness, 87, 89
anger and, 39
Buddhism and, 38
in meditation, 39
Miracle of Tithing, The (Hansen), 147
Miracles, through giving, 7, 32–33

examples of, 8–9, 23
Money, 63–70, 156. *See also* Wealth
attitudes about, 65–67
children's allowance and, 102
exercise on, 66–67
managing, 69–70, 74
tithing, 145–46
want/need difference and, 67–69
Mother Teresa, 28
Motorola, leadership of, 58
MSF. *See* Médecins sans Frontières

Nasruddin, 28–29
Natural disaster, of tsunami, 1–2
Needs, of humans, 25–28
Negative attitudes, 171
Negative emotions, 170
Nightingale, Earl, 31
Nonprofit organizations, 114–19
authors and, 46–47
in community, 114–17
evaluation of, 143–44
giving to, 46–47, 114–19, 136–37, 153
needs list for, 136–37
small organizations in, 117–19
types of, 116
Non-Smokers's Rights Association, 118

Oad, Jenny, 61
Omron, 166
Organ donation, 61–62
Oxfam, 113

Pakistan, 24, 113–14
First Micro Finance Bank Ltd program in, 69–70
Parks, Rosa, 112
Pay It Forward (Hyde), 36
Pay It Forward Foundation, 36
People, connection with, 21–22
Physical benefits, of giving, 22–23
endorphin release, 3
longer life, 4
weight loss, 4
PLAN. *See* Planned Lifetime Advocacy Network
Planet, 119–22
Planned giving, 155
Planned Lifetime Advocacy Network (PLAN), 118
Plato, 129
Pluralism, 128

Potential, ability to reach, 23
Power of Hope, 59–60
Princess Margaret Hospital
    as cancer research center, 32–33
    Dove fund-raising campaign for, 33
Priorities, 38, 83, 135, 139
Procter & Gamble, 166
Purpose, in life, 28–30
Putnam, Robert, 21, 61

Regrets, 40, 43–44
Reiter, Mark, 162
Relationship
    with children, 100
    at death, 132
    exercise on, 99
    forgiveness in, 42–43
    gift-giving development of, 10
    healing of, 38, 94–99
    honesty in, 94, 95
    new, through giving, 20
    regrets in, 40, 43–44
    with spouse, 32, 41–42, 67, 93–96
    symbiotic, 10–11
Resources, in giving, 138–39
Respect, 104
    for earth, 154
    giving with, 127–28
Ripple effect, 13–14, 36
Robin, Vicki, 145
Roddick, Anita, 165
Rodriguez, Rolando, 115
Rogers, Fred, 94
Roper Center for Public Opinion, on
        corporation support, 57–58
Rumi, 23, 37, 129

Sacrifice, 38–40
Sanders, Tim, 50–51
Schuller, Robert, 127
Segal, Jerome M., 144
Self, 86–91
    centeredness, reduction of, 21
    finding, 30–32
    giving break to, 88–89
    giving to, 86–91, 132–33
    inner voice and, 87–88
    learning to help, 90–91
Self-actualization, 25–27
"Servant Leadership," 161–62
7 Habits of Highly Effective People, The,
        (Covey), 41, 81

7UP documentary film, 88
Seven Steps to Lasting Happiness (Jamal), 63
Sheth, Jagdish N., 161
Sisodia, Rajendra S., 161
Skills, 70–74
    building of, 72–73
    exercise for, 73
    sharing of, 71–72
Small organizations, 117–19
Social conscious policies, of corporations, 57
Social involvement, 19, 107–8, 110–12
Social Venture Partners (SVP), 148
Socrates, 144
Soul, giving as exercise for, 20
Soul of a Citizen: Living with Conviction in a
        Cynical Time (Loeb), 101, 107
Soul of Money, The (Twist), 67
South Africa, 111
Speed of Trust, The (Covey and Merrill), 164
Spouse
    giving to, 93–99
    relationship with, 32, 41–42, 67,
        93–96
    time with, 94
SPUD, 163–64
Squires, Conrad, 53
Starbucks, 161, 162
Sufis, 60, 133, 168
Suicide, 61
Survival Is Not Enough: Why Smart
        Companies Abandon Worry and
        Embrace Change (Godin), 49
Suzuki, David, 120
Suzuki, Severn, 121
SVP. See Social Venture Partners
Symbiotic relationship, 10–11

Tannen, Deborah, 81
Television
    fear increase through, 21
    Marx on, 51
    turning off of, 51–52, 171
    volunteer work reduced by, 51
Time, 62–64, 156
    for children, 100
    exercise for, 64
    with family, 63
    management of, 63
    with spouse, 94
    tithing, 146–47
    volunteer work as tithing of, 146–47
Tipping Point, The (Gladwell), 12

Tithing
    idea, 147–48
    intrapersonal, 148–51
    money, 145–46
    time, 146–47
Tomlin, Lily, 148
Touch, 75–77
    children and, 75–76
    massage and, 76
    violence and, 76
Tragedy, laughter and, 45–47
Twist, Lynne, 67

Unconditional love, 38–39, 42, 105
UNHCR. See United Nations High
    Commission for Refugees
UNICEF, 113
United Nations High Commission for
    Refugees (UNHCR), 113
United Network for Organ Sharing, 62
UPS, 162

van Nostrand, Caroline, 33
Van Seters, David, 164
Violence, 7
    touch and, 76
Volunteer work, 24
    American Health on, 22
    of authors, 11–12, 23–24
    health improvement through, 4, 22
    leadership and, 55–56
    life expectancy and, 22
    television reduction of, 51
    as time tithing, 146–47

Vondeling, Johanna, 71
Voss, Carla, 167

Ward, William Arthur, 56
Wealth, 30–31, 68
    Bush's tax cut and, 154
Web sites
    LAUGHS, 44
    www.livingdonorsonline.org, 61
    www.powerofgiving.org, 135
West, Cornel, 30
What Got You Here Won't Get You There
    (Goldsmith and Reiter), 162
When the Body Says No: Understanding the
    Stress-Disease Connection (Maté),
    49–50
Who Dies? An Investigation of Conscious
    Living and Conscious Dying (Levine
    and Levine), 50
Wisdom, 52–53
Wolfe, David B., 161
Workplace, 3
Write for Rights campaign, 166–67

Xerox, 165

Yahgulanaa, Michael Nicoll, 61
Yahoo, Sanders of, 50
You Just Don't Understand: Women and Men
    in Conversation (Tannen), 81
Your Money or Your Life: Transforming
    Your Relationship with Money and
    Achieving Financial Independence
    (Dominguez and Robin), 144–45

About the Authors

Azim Jamal is an international inspirational speaker and the chairman and founder of Corporate Sufi Worldwide, Inc. (www.corporatesufi.com), a company which specializes in helping individuals and corporations to unleash potential and regain balance by blending Sufi and contemporary philosophers. A former professional accountant, Jamal holds three professional accounting qualifications and has been a senior partner in an accounting firm for over fifteen years. He decided to make the switch from "accounting for business" to "accounting for life" after a life-changing experience volunteering in the developing world. In 2003, Azim received the SPARK Award from the Canadian Association of Professional Speakers Vancouver Chapter. He lives in Vancouver, Canada, with his wife, parents, and two children.

Harvey McKinnon is one of North America's top fundraising experts. An inspirational speaker, author, and trainer, he has helped raise hundreds of millions of dollars for nonprofits from Amnesty International to the Canadian Cancer Society to UNICEF. His fund-raising consulting company, Harvey McKinnon Associates (www.harveymckinnon.com), works for a wide variety of causes in Canada and the USA. He has produced several award-winning documentary films, including *Side by Side: Women Against AIDS*, *The Black Sea in Crisis*, and *The Nature of David Suzuki*. He is a cofounder of Amuleta Computer Security. He has served on many boards for both business and nonprofits. He knows at least 13,657 jokes. Harvey lives with his family in Vancouver, Canada.

The Tides Foundation and **Tides Canada** are nonprofit organizations that promote social justice, economic opportunity, and a sustainable environment across North America. The authors shall donate to Tides Foundation/Tides Canada a portion of any profits that they earn from their publication of this book.